UITGAVEN VAN HET
NEDERLANDS HISTORISCH-ARCHAEOLOGISCH INSTITUUT TE ISTANBUL

Publications de l'Institut historique-archéologique néerlandais de Stamboul
sous la direction de
E. VAN DONZEL, Machteld J. MELLINK,
C. NIJLAND et J.J. ROODENBERG

LVIII

A SURVEY IN NORTHEASTERN SYRIA

A SURVEY IN NORTHEASTERN SYRIA

by

DIEDERIK J.W. MEIJER
University of Amsterdam

NEDERLANDS HISTORISCH-ARCHAEOLOGISCH INSTITUUT
TE ISTANBUL
1986

I.S.B.N. 90 6258 058 0
Printed in Belgium

TABLE OF CONTENTS

A SURVEY IN NORTHEASTERN SYRIA *

1.0 Supported by grants from the Faculty of Letters of the University of Amsterdam, the writer undertook an archaeological surface survey in Northeast Syria during the months of September in 1976, 1977 and 1979 [1]. The area surveyed is situated in the Muḥāfiẓa of Ḥassaka and is defined by

to the north:	the Turko-Syrian border
to the south:	the main track Tell Brāk, Ḥaṣawīya F., Bab al Ḥadīd, Malkīya, ʿAyn Dīwār
to the east:	the Syro-Iraqi border
to the west:	the asphalt road Qamishlī-Ḥassaka.

1.1 *Geomorphology*. The area under consideration has two main geomorphological aspects: much of it is undulating proluvial and alluvial-proluvial plain with shallow erosion valleys, while in the north there are middle quaternary and more recent alluvial fans, rolling hills dissected by erosion, and lava plateaus. The soils consist of continental conglomerates, sandstone, limestone [2], clay marl and tuff-breccia; in the northeast basalts are ubiquitous [3]. Probably because of intensive irrigation both north and south of the present border the marshy areas indicated on the old maps are virtually all dried up or drained the year round, and the wadis carry very little water [4]. The main ones, i.e. the Djaghdjagh, the Djarrāḥ and the Khanzīr

* This text formed part of the writer's doctoral dissertation titled *Aspects of Syro-Mesopotamian Archaeology. Excavation, Syrvey and Iconography (University of Amsterdam, 1984)*. Only few changes have been possible since december 1983. I am very grateful to my promotor, Professor Maurits van Loon, for his expert guidance, his patience and his friendship. Professor Machteld Mellink (Bryn Mawr) gave very useful advice on the final form of this manuscript, which places me in her debt. Any inaccuracies of course remain the author's responsibility.

[1] Heartfelt gratitude is hereby extended to the Syrian Directorate of Antiquities and Museums, especially to Dr. Afif Bahnassi, Director-General, and to Dr. Adnan Bounni, Director of Excavations, for permitting and supporting this undertaking. Also Dr. Kassem Toueir and Dr. Nassib Saliby deserve our warmest thanks for their unbounded cooperation; Mr. S. Yunān and the late M. al Muṭlaq were very helpful in the field as the Directorate's representatives. Finally we express our gratitude to the inhabitants of the region, who were friendly, hospitable and interested in our work.
The technical preparation of this report has greatly benefitted from the invaluable help of many people. Mr. Jan de Wit drew the sherds, on which Mrs. G. Wild-Wülker and Mr. R. Leenders did preliminary work. Mr. P. Akkermans Jr. drew the obsidian and flint objects. Mrs. I. de Graaf typed the manuscript. Printing the pottery drawings was the work of Mr. M. Bootsman. Mr. W.H. van Soldt gave valuable Assyriological advice, and Dr. J.D. Hawkins kindly provided the note on the tablet (p. 44f.).

[2] Apparently limestone provided the main source for the tempering of pottery clays; cf. section 6 on the pottery.

[3] Ponikarov 1966.

[4] Only the more important wadis have been indicated in figure 1.

are perennial streams. In antiquity dry farming may have been possible in the northeastern part of the region, if one may judge from the present annual precipitation, which there fluctuates between 400-600 mm (Wirth 1971: 92 and map 3). The southwest half of the region receives 300-400 mm per annum. The major crops at present are wheat, barley, cotton and water melon. Oil drilling has recently become an important industry in the northeastern part of Syria's 'Panhandle', centering around a new town called Rumaylān (not to be confused with Tall Rumaylān, site no. 154). Sheep and goats are herded by the inhabitants, whose numbers have grown through the immigration of 'Maghmurīn' ('inundated ones'), i.e. former inhabitants of the area now covered by Lake Assad.

2.0 *Origin and Purpose.* The plan for research in the area originated during a graduate seminar on the Archaeology of the Old Assyrian Period held in 1975-1976 at the Archaeological-Historical Institute of the University of Amsterdam. It was felt that the area might *a.* provide a pottery sequence that would include assemblages of the Middle Bronze Age, against the background of which for instance the so-called 'Ḫabūr Ware' (cf. Hamlin 1971)[5] could be placed; b. furnish evidence to aid interpretation of the archives of the Old Assyrian merchants as well as other textual sources[6]. Upon arrival on the scene in 1976 the number of *talls* proved to be much larger than had been expected on the basis of the available literature. Consequently, as it was foreseen that money and time would be insufficient to cover the entire area east of the Djaghdjagh (the original target area), a geographically well-defined smaller region was chosen (see 1.0), leaving additional areas to be surveyed in the future[7].

3.0 *History of Research in the Area* Although the great number of mounds attest to the attraction that the area had for settlers, modern archaeology has only hesitantly set foot there. Early travellers mention the area in a general sense: e.g. de Thevenot 1682, Layard 1853, Sachau 1883, de Perthuis 1896, Oppenheim 1899,

[5] At the time of writing, J. N. Tubb's Ph.D. Thesis (University of London, Institute of Archaeology) entitled "The Development of Painted Pottery in Syria during the Early Second Millennium BC" was not available.

[6] Recent excavations at Tall Laylān (no. 44, cf. Weiss 1981/2) have since rendered the identification of that site with Šubat Enlil probable.

[7] Dr. Kate Fielden has since completed a D.Phil. Dissertation (as yet unpublished) incoporating the results of a survey along the southern Djaghdjagh and Wadi Raḍḍ stretches. (I thank Miss Fielden for her courtesy in sending me part of the manuscript). For the Tübingen survey of the Lower Khabūr, cf. Archiv für Orientforschung 25 1977 249-255; AfO 26 1978 181-195. For a survey west of the Djaghdjagh, see Davidson and McKerrell 1976. A cursory survey through part of our area was undertaken by A. Dobel, W. van Liere and A. Maḥmud, cf. Archiv für Orientforschung 25 1974-77: 259-264.

Bell 1911, Sarre and Herzfeld 1911, Dussaud 1927; more specific mention is found in, e.g., Poidebard 1934, van Liere 1955, Moortgat 1959, Dillemann 1962 and Davidson and McKerrell 1976. Excavations or soundings were effected at Brāk (Mallowan 1936, 1937 and 1947, Oates 1982) and recently at Tall Laylān (Weiss 1981/2) and at Tall Barrī (Pecorella and Salvini 1981/2)[8]. An unpublished manuscript of Mallowan's, reçounting results of a cursory survey on the area, is deposited in the British Museum[9], but was not seen by this writer. Of the works mentioned, especially those of Dillemann and Poidebard are useful. The latter gives important photographs (cf., e.g., pl. 120 for the importance of the Djaghdjagh earlier this century). Whereas relevant information from these sources is quoted under the individual sites, it is worth noting here that Poidebard mentions (1934:162) a "ville fortifiée située à XXXIII M.P. de Nisibin (pl. CLX, 3)", which we were unable to find: also 'Sarbane = Serwān', some 39 km. east of Nisibin may be Serfan, now in Turkey (ca. 46° 26′ 50″ E.L.). Davidson and McKerrell name only a selection of the sites they visited (1976: 48-49, see also note 7).

4.0 *Method.* Sites were located in the following manner: each morning the team[10] drove from the base (in Qamishilī) to a specific sector measuring approximately 20 sqkm., and defined by modern tracks. There the immediately visible mounds or remains were visited; starting from these, other sites were looked for more or less systematically on foot. Local inhabitants were questioned about the presence of ancient remains—information that was always gladly provided and often led to valuable finds. In this way more than 300 sites were located and plotted on the map. The more important of these were measured and drawn by the steps-and-sighting-compass method[11], keeping to approximately the same elevation. The resulting plans (mostly 1:2000) are necessarily imprecise but do give a general impression of layout and orientation[12]. Elevations above the level of the surrounding fields were measured with a leveling instrument. If a mound was smaller than ca. 100 × 100 × 6 m., measurements were estimated, especially if the entire surface

[8] Important references in these accounts to sites covered by the survey are mentioned in the site catalogue.

[9] Fielden (n. 7:232); cf. Kühne 1980 n. 5.

[10] Without the much appreciated help of the following persons the work could not have been done: Mrs. Y. Telenga, Mr. P. Gesner van der Voort, Mr. A. Koelman, Mr. H. den Boer and the representatives Mr. Yunān and Mr. al Muṭlaq. Their good humour when faced each morning with the same dreary routine tasks was truly amazing!

[11] Ca. 1-m. paces (always taken by the same person) are counted and directed towards a given point in the field of which the bearing on the compass has first been established and noted; this procedure is repeated around the *tall* until the original point of departure is reached again. The distances thus paced off are at least consistent.

[12] The aspect of especially small mounds may change considerably over short periods due to excavations made for *libn*.

was covered by a modern village. Photographs and/or colour slides were taken of the more important (i.e. larger) sites, and a record was kept of such data as source of water, present means of subsistence, presence of modern cemeteries, of a topographic marker, accessibility and availability of rooms or houses to be rented by an expedition. At all sites the surface was examined for pottery sherds and other finds, these being collected at ca. 1 m. intervals (but there was no strict adherence to a grid). The sherds were sorted in a preliminary fashion. Feature sherds (i.e. rims, bases and decorated sherds) wer kept [13], the remainder discarded on the spot after notes had been taken.

4.1. *Maps*. Unfortunately, no air photographs could be obtained. For the location of sites we used the Qamis͟hlī-Sind͟jār 1:200.000 map (1950) and the Qara D͟jūq Dag͟h 1:200.000 map (1945). Although this scale was not perfectly suited to the purpose, all sites could be mapped with reasonable accuracy. When doubt arose, sites were sighted from three different locations indicated on the maps, resulting in dependable triangulation. Few important inaccuracies were found on the maps. They regarded placenames, stretches of wadi or the location of sites on either bank. At present a secondary asphalt road, not indicated on the maps we used, runs approximately along D͟hibāna (site no. 181) - Arbāṭ (163) - Ṭuwayyil (193) - Quṣayyib (196) and Abū Tuwayna (212); south of the latter it crosses the Ḥaṣawīya-Brāk track. It is not indicated on fig. 1.

The plan to include contour lines in figure 1 has been abandoned, since the map would have become unreadable, and because the base map is widely available.

4.2 *Orthography*. Apart from the majority, who speak Arabic, there are Turkish- and Kurdish speaking inhabitants as well as a few 'Assyrians' in the region, who together are responsible for a bewildering mixture of names for sites. In addition, the maps sometimes give erroneous or antiquated names. Transliteration of spoken place-names involves a certain amount of interpretation, which, for one not vey well versed in the local Arabic, Kurdish and Turkish dialects, may entail misinterpretation. To impose some unity on the mixture, the system of transliteration of the *Encyclopaedia of Islam* is used here for the Arabic names, with the exception of the ḳ, which is here transcribed as q; the feminine *nisbe* ending is given as -iya.

[13] The writer is grateful to the Syrian Antiquities Department for permission to take a sample of the finds to Amsterdam, where they are accessible to those interested.

5.0 *The sites.* The sites are listed in the order in which they were visited, with a set of data following each site number.

Name(s):	small sites often have no name and are called "X" here; large sites sometimes have 2 or 3 names, often in more than one language.
Measurements:	in meters, first *length*, then *width* (both taken at the base of the mound), then *height*.
D.	Means a measured *plan* was made (cf. 4.0), most of which are not published here (but see fig. 6). Only one contour was drawn in these cases, at an elevation taken to be representative of the base of the mound.
F.	Means a *photograph* was taken. Only a few of these are published here (figs. 2-5).
V.	Indicates that *village* houses now cover all or part of the mound, to such a degree as to hinder archaeological work.
C.	As *V*, but pertaining to a (relatively recent) *cemetery*.
P.	*Pottery*. Code-numbers from 1-14 have been used to indicate the various pottery cultures and/or periods. For details the reader is referred to section 6.3. "!" indicates a dense concentration.
R.	Signifies *remarks* of a varying nature: other finds such as seals or flint, chert and obsidian; mention by other sources (not exhaustive); identification with historical sites, etc.

NB: The modern towns of Qamishlī, Bāb al Ḥadīd, ʿAyn Dīwār and Malkīya (Dīrīk) have not been included in the survey, although all four contain important ancient remains. The area between Samīḥa (269b) and Tall Brāk was not surveyed by us, as it belonged to 'Miss Fielden's territory' (cf. note 7).

5.1 *Site Catalogue*

1 GRA-i RESH / TALL AṢWAD. 160 × 100 × 10 m. D.F.
P. 7, 9a, 13.
R. Not to be confused with the Grai Resh excavated by S. Lloyd (cf. Iraq VII 1940:13ff.).

2 NAʿMATLĪ. 80 × 50 × 7 m. V.
P. 9.

3 TALL KHARNŪB. NOT VISITED.

4 TALL al SHAʿĪR. 300 × 220 × 29 m. D.F.
P. 9, 9a.
R. Probably = "Shair" on Mallowan's fig. 1 in IRAQ III 1936. Cf. Sachau 1883:389.

5 DŪGĒR. 500 × 300 × 26 m. D.F.
P. 7-9, 12.
R. Complex mound with three summits (A easternmost, 26 m., B 18 m., C 5 m.) in a northeast-southwesterly configuration. Summits of B and C have modern graves. Summit of A shows remains of a rectagular mud brick building with a main room of ca. 13 × 9.5 m., thickness of walls ca. 80 cm., which dates to ca. 1950 AD. See Dillemann 1962 map VIII (Dougueur).

6 TALL BA(YA)NDŪR. 260 × 160 × 12 m. D.F.
P. 7(?), 7a, 9, 9a.
R. During a second visit a local farmer showed a statuette reportedly found on the tall. Brown limestone, height 32 cm., frontal width 16 cm. See fig. 7c. For comparisons, see Th. H. Carter, Expedition XII 1970 22-40, esp. p. 29. (Sinjar 1). Prob. LB. See Dillemann 1962 map VIII and p. 80 n. 3.

7 TALL KHATŪN. 100 × 80 × 9 m. D.F.V.
P. 2, 9a.
R. Old basalt-lined well at NE edge of mound, now filled up with dirt.

8 TALL al SAYYID / GARDĒM. 130 × 100 × 8 m. D.F.V.
P. 9, 9a, 10.

9 SHALḤUMĪYA. h. ca. 4 m. NOT VISITED. V.

10 MAḤARQĀN. V. diam. ca. 100 m.
P. 13, 14.
R. Christian church.

10a KIRKĪ SHĀMŪ. NOT VISITED.
Cf. Sachau 1883:389.

11 QAḤṬANĪYA / QUBŪR al BĪḌ. F.V.
P. 4.
R. Mound south of asphalt road, heavily damaged by old French barracks built of basalt, and subsequent libn mining.

12 TALL SAʿDIYA / GARDĒM. 250 × 200 × 19 m. D.F.C.
P. 7, 9, 9a, 13.

13 KHAZIMŪK. 120 × 70 × 6 m. C.
P. 13.
R. Mound lies ca. 2 km. west of village Khazimūk.

14 DAYR AYYŪB. 300 × 200 × 23 m. D.F.
P. 8-12.
R. Complex mound with highest summit to the south, on which remains of a modern, rectangular mud brick building with basalt foundations and cement floors, oriented N-S. Two water springs. A neo-Assyrian linear style cylinder seal was shown by the inhabitants ('not to be photographed'), depicting a

winged quadruped with young, two standing human figures, and a star. Size ca. 3 × 1,5 cm., made of dark veined stone. = Dillemann 1962 'Derouna Kolunga' (map VIII)??

15 TALL ḤADJAR / GIRBKĒL (formerly TALL MANṢŪR). 300 × 200 × 22 m. D.F.V.
P. 2, 3, 8, 9, 14.

16 TALL MA'SHŪQ. 160 × 140 × 19 m. D.F.
P. 2, 3, 9.
R. Mound is partly natural.

17 QAṬRANĪYA / BŪR SA'ĪD. 150 × 130 × 8 m. D.F.
P. 13, 14.

18 ḤALIMŪK. 70 × 70 × 3 m. F.
P. 8, 9, 9a.
R. Remains of a (basalt) foundation podium?

19 TALL TAWQAL. 50 × 40 × 3 m. F.C.
P. 9a.

20 TALL YAHŪD. Ca. 60 × 50 × 3 m. F.
P. 13, 14.
R. Lies ca. 1500 m. south of no. 19, reachable on foot only. Mound is mostly natural.

21 DAYR UNĀ AGHĀ / DAYR GHUṢN. 320 × 260 × 30 m. D.F.
P. 9a, 14.
R. On the summit the basalt foundations and remains of the mud brick superstructure of a building (16 × 11.5 m.) on a podium to the western and southern end of which walls abut enclosing a rectangular yard of ca. 29 × 29 m. Supposed to have been a French police station; = Derouna (Dillemann 1962:132 and map VIII). Sachau 1883:385.

22 ḤASHNĪYA. 30 × 30 × 2 m.
P. 9, 14.

23 TALL MEHUM / MUHIM. 280 × 200 × 17 m. D.F.
P. 2, 3, 5, 6, 7, 9, 9a, 14.

24 TALL 'ABRA. 320 × 300 × 18 m. D.F.V.
P. 8, 9.
R. Poidebard (1934:160, pl. 159) mentions a Castellum and an Enceinte Assyrienne at 'Abra Fūqānī. The latter is probably to be identified with 'Alī Kūz on the 1945 1:200.000 map, although local inhabitants only knew that name. The original plan to return to the site ascertain the extent of Poidebard's observations, no traces of which could be found during our first visit, could unfortunately not be implemented. The present 'Abra (our

no. 24) is to be identified as ʿAbra Taḥtānī. Cf. Dillemann 1962 map VIII (there the course of the wadi is slightly incorrect). Cf. also U. Moortgat-Correns, Die Bildwerke vom Djebelet al Bēdā (Berlin 1972), Karte II.

24a ʿALĪ KŪZ, prob. = ʿAbra FAWQĀNĪ (cf. no. 24) 50 × 40 × 3 m. F.V.
P. 9a, 14.
R. See no. 24.

25 GHAFQĪYA / BADJĀNĪ. 160 × 130 × 14 m. D.F.
P. 2-4.
R. Southwest of the mound a low extension produced a few weathered, indeterminable (modern?) sherds. The extension may be natural.

26 TALL LUKS. 200 × 140 × 9 m. (max., north side). D.F.
P. 9.
R. Part of mound must be natural. A basin with drainage gullet, made of basalt, lay on the north western end of the mound.

27 QUNAYṬRA. 160 × 100 × 20 m. D.F.
P. 13, 14, (5a, see AfO 26 1978/9 p. 162).
R. Situated on the left bank of the Wadī Bāb al Ḥadīd which has locally been turned into a reservoir, drowning, according to the local villagers, a 'white marble bridge' presumably of Late Roman times. A pit lined with baked brick is visible on the northern side of the mound. Leading up to the near-by village are remains of a Roman road, cf. Poidebard 1934:166 and pl. 161^{2}?? After our passage in 1976 a small sounding was made by Dr. A. Mahmud, cf. AfO 26 1978/9 162. In 1977 a farmer showed us a white chalcedony stamp seal (fig. 8^{b}). A smaller knoll just south of this mound produced no sherds.

28 KARAKILISE. 100 × 100 × 20 m. F.
P. 13, 14.
R. Hill is partly natural.

29 GRA-i DERĀ / TALL al MIḌRĪ / TALL al DAYR. F.
P. 14, 15.
R. Natural hill with remains of a main rectangular and two side buildings, built of hewn dark basalt (main building ashlar masonry). Supposed to have been a monastery.

30 SĒ GERKA. ca. 100 × 100 × 6 m.
P. 13-15.
R. See Dillemann 1962 map V "Seguirká", and p. 38 and 83 n. 2. Heavily disturbed by excavations for mud brick.

31 KHIRBAT al QAṬA. ca. 80 × 60 × 3 m. F.
P. 14.
R. Ruins of recent basalt buildings.

32 GHASĀNĪYA / QARGHŪ. 190 × 120 × 18 m. D.F.
P. 9, 9a.
R. See Dillemann 1962 map VIII "Kergo".

33 TALL ḤALLĀQ. 180 × 160 × 10 m. D.
P. 5a, 9, 9a.

34 TALL 'AWAR / GĒR DHABBĀN. 100 × 100 × 7 m. V.
P. 9, 14.

35 DJABRĪYA. 100 × 80 × 7 m. V.
P. 14.

36 KIRK KHAZNA. NOT VISITED.

37 TALL DJAMMĀL. 180 × 120 × 12 m. D.F.V.C.
P. 9, 9a.
R. There are low projections of the mound on the northern and northwestern side, with the same pottery.

38 MA'BADA. ca. 80 × 80 × 5 m. V.C.
P. 8-10.

39 TALL AṢFAR (I) / SHAYKH GUNDUK. 250 × 160 × 10(-3) m. D.F.
P. 13, 14.
R. Main mound is partly natural. West of its lies another small mound now covered by modern houses. To the north is a low projection of the main mound. Very little pottery, no chert.

40 TALL AṢFAR (II). ca. 80 × 80 × 2 m. V.
P. 9a.

41 QAṢR al DĪB. 250 × 220 × 17 m. D.F.V. See fig. 2a.
P. 9, 9a, 11, 14.
R. Much basalt used for ancient terracing walls. French fortress on top, in ruins.

42 MIR 'AZAZIĀT. ca. 70 × 50 × 3 m.
P. 1.

43 TALL ṢAḤĪYA (map Ṣamīya). 150 × 100 × 25 m. F.
P. 9, 9a.
R. Much higher on west side than on east side, due to slope of fields towards wadi.

44 TALL LAYLĀN. F.V.
P. 5-10.
R. Mounds were not measured here, as subsequent excavations were foreseen; these were started in 1979 by H. Weiss (Yale, USA). One of the largest mounds in the region. Western gate in (outlying) city wall shows traces of burning (ca. 2100 BC?). Eastern city area produced baked mud brick as well

as pottery slag (misfired stack of bowls, cf. fig. 18r). Alabaster sherd with Egyptian hieroglyphs (cf. fig. 7, and p. 41). See Poidebard 1934 pl. 160; van Liere 1963 for sketch of layout; Weiss 1981/2.

45a "TALL DJISR" / TALL GHAYDA(?). ca 70 × 40 × 10 m. F.
P. 7a, 8, 9, 14.
R. Across the river a slightly larger *tall*, flattened at the top, probably served, like our No. 45a, as a bridge head, but could not be visited as it lies on Turkish soil; = "Hügel" on sketch Sachau 1883:379.

b DJAZĪRAT IBN 'UMAR. F. See figs. 4, 5.
R. Stone bridge-pylons; one arc still intact. Date, at least of part, Selçuk. One pylon has eight faces of white sand stone relief set in the basalt down stream end of the pylon, depicting personified sun, moon, wind, etc. Cf. Poidebard 1934: pl. 158; Dillemann 1962: pl. XI[d]; Ilter 1974: pl. XVI-XVIII, figs. 2-3; Çulpan 1975:44-48 + lit; Preusser WVDOG 17 1911:24-28. pls. 37-40.

c GRAVE of a holy man (Islamic), built of ashlar masonry; a lower podium-wall carries two registers of inscription on its black basalt blocks, a higher one has one register of same on slightly larger, alternating black and white basalt blocks.

46 SHŪTĪ. 240 × 180 × 3 m. D.F.V.
P. 8, 9, 9a.

47 QAṢĪR. 220 × 160 × 11 m. D.F.V.
P. 9, 10.

48 ḤAMŪ. 100 × 100 × 6 m. V.
P. 13.

49 TALL BARĪSH. 250 × 160 × 16 m. D.F.
P. 9, 9a, 10.
R. Mound has long extension at southern end.

50 QABR AḤMAD al SAHĪM ca. 50 × 50 × 4 m.
P. 13, 14.
R. Islamic grave monument on small regular mound; three obsidian blade fragments, one core flake.

51 TALL NIṢR. 360 × 250 × 20 m. D.F.
P. 9a, 10, 12, 14.
R. Long 'tail' at southern end.

52 SHĪBANĪYAT DAḤḤĀM. 170 × 150 × 10 m. D.F.V.
P. 9, 9a, 14.
R. Some islamic blue glass fragments.

53 TALL BALĪDJ. 310 × 200 × 24 m. D.F.C.
P. 4-9a, 12, 13.

54 KHIRBAT DĪBA. diam. ca. 100 m. V.
P. 13, 14.

55 BAYĀZA. (I). Height 3 m.
P. 14.
R. Name by association with next village (no. 56a).

56a BAYĀZA. (II). ca. 100 × 80 × 4 m. V.
P. 8.
R. Northwest of present track, southeast of Wādī ʿAbbās.

56b BAYĀZA KABĪRA. ca. 100 × 100 × 6 m. V.
P. 7, 7a, 8, 9, 9a.
R. A few unworked obsidian flakes.

57 BAYĀZA ṢAGHĪRA. ca. 80 × 80 × 5 m. V.
P. 7, 7a, 8.
R. South of railroad track, north of wadi (crossing by bridge at Bayāza Kabīra (no. 56b).

58 ABŪ ḤUDJAYRA. 260 × 110 × 6 m. D.F.V.
P. 2, 3, 7, 9a.
R. Situated on a natural stone outcrop.

59 SHŪRAK. 210 × 120 × 7 m. D.F.V.
P. 9, 14.
R. South of modern asphalt road. Name on 1945 map Muzayrīb. Davidson and McKerrell 1976 no. 13?

60 TANNŪRĪYA. ca.100 × 100 × 4 m. V.
P. Dense modern habitation obstructed sherd collecting.

61 BUWAYYIR. ca. 80 × 60 × 3 m. D.F.V.
P. 2, 3, 4.
R. South of the main tall a low rise contains modern graves. See Dillemann 1962 map VIII ("Boueira").

62 KHIRBAT KHALĪL. 100 × 100 × 3 m. V.
P. cf. no. 60.

63a KHAZNA KABĪRA. 220 × 140 × 13 m. D.F.V.
P. 1, 2, 3, 13, 14.
b R. Slightly to the SSW lies Tall al Iskandar (ca. 40 × 30 × 2 m.) which, according to the inhabitants of Khazna, contains Christian burials. The NW side of the main mound reportedly contains a baked-brick arch (Byzantine or Ottoman?) discovered during *libn* mining. Not visible, as pit was subsequently filled in again for safety reasons. See Dillemann 1962 map VIII ("Ghazna").

64 KHAZNA ṢAGHĪRA. ca. 80 × 60 × 4m. F.C.
P. 13, 14.
R. Very gradual slopes and lack of features made a contour drawing impractical. Perhaps the site was walled(?), for the north and southwest slight rises in the ground are just barely visible. Measurements given are those of the main mound.

65 SUḤAYYIL. ca. 100 × 100 × 4 m. F.V.
P. 13, 14.
R. Probably same as "Souḥeilé", cf. Dussaud 1927 map XV.

66 KHIRBAT KHAZNA / TULŪL KHAZNA. ca. 60 × 50 × 4 m. (both).
P. 13, 14.

67 "X". ca. 80 × 80 × 3 m. F.
p. 9a.
R. Some burnt brick.

68 "X". ca. 50 × 50 × 1 m.
P. 1, 11.
R. Fragment of a basalt pestle.

69 KHARAYDJKA (I). 70 × 70 × 2 m.
P. 8, 9.
R. This moundlet lies just south of the village Kh. (no. 70).

70 KHARAYDJKA (II). ca. 100 × 100 × 5 m. V.
P. Too intensively inhabited for sherd collecting.

71 "X". 150 × 80 × 3 m.
P. 2-5, 7, 7a, 9a.
R. Fragment of a basalt quern and a limestone basin.

72 GĒR SAWWĀR / TALL SAWWĀR / TALL FURSĀN. 320 × 160 × 23 m.
P. 7, 7a, 8, 9, 9a, 11, 12.
R. Perhaps = Dillemann 1962 map VIII "Kerou"?

73 GUNDUK. 70 × 60 × 2 m.
P. 7, 8, 9.

74 SĪḤĀ. 250 × 200 × 4 m.
P. Too intensively inhabited for sherd collecting.

75 KHARĀB al BAGHĀL. 80 × 60 × 3 m. C.
P. 11, 12, 13, 14.

76 "X". ca. 60 × 50 × 2 m.
P. 13.
R. A low ridge almost connects nos. 75 and 76.

77 "X". ca. 50 × 50 × 2 m.
P. 14.

78 "SĪḤĀ ṢAGHĪRA". ca. 40 × 40 × 1 m.
P. None.
R. Lies in track from the villages Siḥā Kabīra (west) to S. Ṣaghīra (east).

79 QUṬBA TAḤTĀNĪ. 150 × 150 × 3 m. V.
P. 9a.

80 TALL BURHUM. 120 × 80 × 7 m. F.C.
P. 4, 9, 9a.

81 "X". 50 × 40 × 1 m.
P. 14.

82 GĒR SHIRĀN. 240 × 160 × 14 m. D.F.
P. 4, 6, 7, 7a, 9a.

83 "X". 150 × 100 × 2 m.
P. 7, 8, 14.
R. Some chert blades; *libn* mining; garbage dump for Qubūr al Bīḍ.

84 "X". 110 × 100 × 3 m. F.C.
P. 13, 14.
R. Small muslim chapel; squarish fired bricks have been used for the modern graves — these were taken from a ruined building some 20 m. south-southeast of the cemetery.

85 QĪRŪ. 170 × 120 × 6 m. D.
P. 2, 7, 7a, 9.
R. Local tradition has it that the German railroad builders had a camp here in the beginning of this century.

86 "X". ca. 50 × 50 × 1 m.
P. 9, 9a.

87 "TALL NAṢRAN". 70 × 50 × 3 m. F.
P. 9, 9a.
R. Lies across the railroad track from the village Naṣrān; villagers say that the French used to occupy the site.

88a "X". ca. 100 × 100 × 3 m.
P. 3, 4.
R. Part of mound has been dug away; noteworthy is an excavation of 5 × 3 × 1.5 m. with straight sides, providing a section showing ash layers. Immediately southeast of this tall lies 88 b.

88b "X". ca. 50 × 50 × 1 m.
P. 14.

89 SHIBĀK. 150 × 100 × 4 m.
P. 9, 9a.

90 SHĪBANĪYA al DJANŪBĪYA / SHĪBANĪYAT DANDAḤ. ca. 150 × 80 × 3 m.
P. 10, 11.

91a TALL MAʿRŪF.
P. 14, 15.
R. Mound containing modern burials from the village. Village itself not noticeably elevated above fields.
Name on 1945 map is Baʿrūr.

91b "TALL MAʿRŪF". ca.60 × 60 × 2 m.
P. 7a, 9.
R. Mound lies 21° SSW from roof of village mosque, distance ca. 1 km.

92 KHIRBAT MAʿRŪF. Overall length ca. 150 m., height ca. 2 m.
P. 3, 4, 6, 7, 9, 9a.
R. Consists of three small mounds in horse-shoe configuration.

93 KUBAYBA. 220 × 120 × 10 m. D.F.
P. 9, 9a.

94 SHARMŪKH. 300 × 200 × 23 m. D.F.
P. 4, 7, 7a.
R. Remains of five parallel brick walls with thick plaster can be seen in the southern bank of the Wādī Buraybidj at 44° ENE from the *tall*'s benchmark.

95 "X". ca. 60 × 50 × 2 m.
P. 10.

96 TALL ABŪ KHAZAF. 340 × 200 × 23 m. D.F.V.
P. 3-9a.
R. Some chert, obsidian and colored glass.

97 "X". ca. 60 m. diameter, height 2 m. C.
P. 14, 15.
R. Cemetery belonging to modern village on no. 96.

98 TALL QARĀṢA. 390 × 280 × 31 m. D.F.C. See fig. 2b.
P. 7-10, 12, 14.
R. Pottery slags; fragmentary bowl of polished granite; baked bricks (esp. on SE slope); uninscribed basalt stela, ca. 1 × 0.8 × 0.2 m. Cf. Dussaud 1927 map XV. The remains of the Roman bridge south of the site mentioned by Poidebard (1934: 163, pl. 161a) have completely disappeared. See also Dillemann 1962 map VIII; Moortgat 1957: map; van Lierde 1963: 114.

99 al ʿAMRĪ. ca. 120 × 100 × 6 m. V.
P. 9a, 11, 14.
R. There are two villages with this name; the westernmost is the *tall*.

100 KHIRBAT SABĪBA. ca. 60 × 40 × 2 m.
P. 13, 14.

101 MATHLAWTHA ʿARĪḌA. ca. 160 × 100 × 4 m. C.V.
P. 8, 9, 11.

102 NĀʿIDJ. ca. 100 × 70 × 3 m.
P. 9, 9a, 10, 13.

103 "X". ca. 50 × 30 × 1 m.
P. 9.

104 WĀWĪYA. ca. 100 × 60 × 3 m. V.
P. 9, 10.

105 al QAṢR. ca. 80 × 50 × 3 m. V.
P. 9.

106 TALL FARSŪK. ca. 200 × 100 × 14 m. D.F.
P. 2, 4, 5, 6, 7, 7a, 8, 9, 9a.
R. Measurements given are of main mound; it has a low extension to the SW.

107a DJALAQ. ca. 150 × 100 × 4 m. V.
P. 9, 9a.

b "X".ca. 70 × 50 × 2 m.
P. 11.
R. Lies just NE of 107a.

108 ʿARĪḌA FAWQĀNĪ. ca. 150 × 100 × 3 m. V.
P. 8, 9.

109 ḤAMĀRA. 170 × 120 × 11 m. D.F.C.
P. 7, 9, 9a, 10.
R. Baked as well as burnt brick. Walls visible in pits dug for libn.

110 "KHIRBAT ḤAMĀRA". ca. 200 × 100 × 3 m.
P. 4, 9a, 10, 12, 14.
R. (name is our own invention). Measurements given cover the entire extent of what in fact are three low tops. The most northerly has predominantly chalcolithic, the southwestern MB-LB and the southeastern Iron Age and modern wares. Some obsidian blades and scrapers.

111 ʿARĪḌA TAḤTĀNĪ. Height 4 m.
P. 14.

112 "X". 60 × 50 × 2 m.
P. --.

113 KHIRBAT QARĀṢA. ca. 70 × 50 × 3 m.
P. 13.

114 KHIRBAT MARDJĀNĪ. ca. 70 × 70 × 3 m.
P. 13.

115a KHIRBAT DJIḤĀSH. ca. 100 × 60 × 2 m.
P. 11, 13.

b R. Lies immediately east of modern village with same name also lying on low mound, which was too inhabited for sherd collecting. Some flint on 115a.

116 TALL TĀYA. 200 × 170 × 20 m. D.F.V.
P. 9, 9a, 14.
R. Some obsidian blades. Map gives Ṭāyir.

117 KHIRBAT ṢŪFĪYA. ca. 100 × 100 × 3 m.
P. 9.

118 TALL MUḤAMMAD DIYĀB. 400 × 290 × 23 m. D.F.C.
P. 7a, 9, 9a, 10.
R. Pottery slags.

119a GRA-i BRĒ. 240 × 200 × 12 m. D.V.
P. 9, 9a, 14.
R. See Dillemann 1962 map VIII "Guérépéré". No trace of an old bridge, as D. already implies.

b Some 200 m. eastward three low hills contain Khabūr ware (9a).

120a GUNDUK SAYYID. ca. 100 × 100 × 6 m. V.
P. Too intensively inhabited for sherd collecting.

b R. To the northwest lies a small rise, reputedly the modern village's cemetery. Not visited.

121 NABŪʿA. 150 × 100 × 5 m. V.
P. 9-11.

122 TALL WULAYQĪ. 280 × 180 × 11 m. D.F.V.
P. 7, 8, 9.
R. Tall is kidney shaped and has a saddle.

123 WULAYQĪ THARTHARA. ca. 100 × 100 × 3 m. V.
P. 9.

124 TALL ABŪ ḤADJAR. 270 × 230 × 17 m. D.F. See fig. 2c.
P. 9, 9a.
R. See van Liere-Lauffray 1964/5, map: T. Abū Hajeyyer.

125 TALL ABŪ FARʿA. 290 × 220 × 26 m. D.F.V.
P. 8, 9!, 9a!
R. See Dillemann 1962 map VIII: T. Farouah. Low extension on NW. side. Perhaps van Liere's Tall Abū Qādir (1954-5: map, ENE of 'Qarassa') is in fact our no 125? There is a site Tall Abū Qādir south of the track from Umm Kahīf-Ḥaṣawīya.

126 GRA-i MIRKA. 180 × 140 × 16 m. D.F.V.
P. 4, 7, 7a, 9a.

127 QUBŪR ḤARB. ca. 60 × 50 × 2 m.
P. 14.
R. Ruins of modern housing.

128 ʿURAYMISH. ca. 100 × 100 × 2 m. C.
P. 8, 9a.
R. Lies to the NW of village called U.

129 BUSHAYRĪYA. ca. 80 × 70 × 2 m.
P. 8, 9, 9a.

130 TALL ʿABBĀS (I). ca. 100 × 60 × 2 m. C.
P. 9.
R. Some obsidian.

131 TALL ʿABBĀS (II). ca. 150 × 100 × 3 m. V.
P. 9.

132 KHIRBAT al SIMM. ca. 40 × 40 × 2 m. V.
P. 14.

133 MAQRINĀT.
R. Modern village on low mound. Not visited.

134 TALL ṬUWAYYIL. 240 × 170 × 18 m. D.F.V.
P. 7-11.

135 KHIRBAT LAZĀQA. 120 × 100 × 2 m.
P. 14.
R. One unworked obsidian chip.

136 BAZŪNA.
R. Not visited; probably contains ruins of modern farm.

137 LAZĀQA. ca. 130 × 90 × 5 m. V.
P. 7a.

138 ḤAṢURATLĪ. ca. 100 × 100 × 4 m.
P. 14.
R. Lies south of rails, not to the north, as the 1945 map indicates.

139 ʿAWDA. 220 × 160 × 20 m. D.F.
P. 8, 9, 9a, 10.
R. Dillemann 1962 map VIII gives a Tall Roummān here, but that name was unknown to the villagers. There are Christians so perhaps 'Ruman' was used to indicate these?

140 TALI ʿAṬSHĀNA. 360 × 180 × 19 m. D.F.V.C.
P. 2, 3, 9, 9a.
R. Low western extebsion.

141 UMM al RADJĪM. 180 × 150 × 3 m.
P. 9, 13.
R. Old (Byzantine?) well, depth 35 m., stone-lined.

142 ʿAMMARĀT FAWQĀNĪ. ca. 200 × 100 × 2 m.
P. 3, 4.

143 ʿAMMARĀT TAḤTĀNĪ. 120 × 80 × 5 m.
P. 9.

144 QAṢRŪK. 200 × 120 × 8 m. D.F.
P. 9, 9a, 13, 14.
R. Modern cemetery to the west, with Syriac inscriptions on tombstones.

145a QARḤŪ. ca. 80 × 60 × 2 m.
P. 2, 3.

b "X". ca. 70 × 50 × 2 m. C.
P. 13, 14.
R. Sites a and b are situated west and east of Umm Kahīf Fawqānī respectively.

146 TALL ʿALŪ. 350 × 260 × 27 m. D.F. See fig. 2d.
P. 3, 4, 9, 9a, 10, 14.
R. Some obsidian.

147 "X". ca. 60 × 60 × 2 m. C.
P. 13, 14.
R. Human bones, Byzantine rooftiles.

148 GĒRDĒM. 230 × 200 × 22 m. D.F.V.
P. 9, 9a.
R. Late Babylonian button stamp seal, made of serpentine. (No illustration available).

149 al QAṢMĪYA. 200 × 100 × 7 m.
P. 9.

150 USAYMIR. ca. 200 × 100 × 6 m.
P. 10.

151 D̲J̲UWADĪYA / D̲J̲AYL ĀG̲H̲Ā. ca. 150 × 100 × 4 m. V.
P. 9, 9a, 14.
R. Now known exclusively as D̲juwadīya. Probably same as "Ğilaġa" (cf. most recently Kessler 1980: 14 f.). No Assyrian pottery was seen by us.

152 K̲H̲ARĀB BAD̲J̲AR. ca. 200 × 200 × 3 m. V.
P. Mound itself too densely inhabited for sherd collecting, but around the main mound there is 13, 14.
R. Above measurements indicate size of mound together with "enceinte", the remains of a mud brick wall, probably also from Byzantine and/or Ottoman date.

153 "X". 120 × 100 × 6 m. C.
P. 10.

154 TALL RUMAYLĀN (al KABĪR).
P. 4, 7, 7a, 8, 9, 9a, 11.

R. Visited only cursorily, as outside proper area for survey. See Kessler 1980 p. 14 f. and note 74.

155 TALL al HĀDĪ / QAL'AT al HĀDĪ. ca 450 × 350 × 40 m.
P. 9, 9a, 10, 11, 11a, 12.
R. Visited only cursorily, as it lay outside the boundaries of the survey area. A villager found the tablet described on p. 44, cf. fig. 8a.

156 TALL ḤAMŪKAR.
P. a.o. 4, 7, 7a, 9, 9a. No Late Bronze material was noticed, but:
R. Visited only cursorily as outside set boundaries; cf. van Liere and Lauffray 1954/55: 137; van Liere 1963: 114 and 120, where identification with Waššukanni is proposed.

157 TALL BRĀK.
P. R: See Mallowan 1947, Fielden 1981, Oates 1982.

158 number deleted.

159 number deleted.

160 DĪYŪ. ca. 100 × 50 × 5 m.
P. 8, 9, 9a, 13.

161 SALĀM 'ALAYK. ca. 100 × 100 × 7 m. V.
P. 12, 13, 14.
R. Obsidian blade fragments.

162 DJUNAYDĪYA. ca. 150 × 100 × 3 m. V.
P. 14, 15.
R. Mound covered by modern village. Lies ca. 2.5 km. *east* of the position given on the 1945 map.

163 ARBĀṬ. 120 × 90 × 12 m. D.V.C.
P. 2, 3, 4, 6, 7, 9, 9a, 13.
R. Measurements given are those of main mound; outlying area covered with sherds measures ca. 280 × 220 m.; fragm. basalt bowl.

164a "X". ca. 40 × 40 × 1 m.
P. 9.
R. Lies just east of no. 164 b.

b TALL SHAYKH 'ADJĪL. V.
P. 12-14.

165 RAKABĪYA. ca. 150 × 100 × 12 m. V.
P. 13 (a.o. rooftiles).

166 TALL al 'ĪD. ca. 500 m. diameter? F.V.
P. see below.
R. Name on 1945 map incorrectly given as "Ḥāyid"; name in Dillemann 1962: 52 (map V) Ayd. A survey of this important mound was—an

exception in this area—not encouraged by the villagers; hence it is not treated in section 8. Ancient remains consist of four summits, the western one ca. 35 m. high, the eastern (covered by the modern village) ca. 22 m., the southern and northern ones lowish. Pottery: N. 10, W. 8, 9, 9a. S. and E. no pottery collected.

167 TALL BASHARĪYA. ca. 130 × 80 × 13 m. V.
P. 13, 14.
R. Lies ca. 70 m. west of asphalt road not indicated on 1945 map (cf. 4.1). Name of village on that map is Bishrīya.

168 TALL ṬARṬAB ṢAGHĪR. 240 × 180 × 23 m. D.F.
P. 8, 9, 9a, 10.
R. Large portions of mound have been removed for *libn*. See also no. 169. Davidson and McKerrell 1976 no. 101 (*or* = our 169).

169 TALL ṬARṬAB KABĪR. 320 × 200 × 35 m. D.F.V.
P. 7, 7a, 9, 10.
R. See for both nos. 168 and 169 also Poidebard 1934:147 and Dillemann 1962: 167 map V. There is a small rise east of no. 169 containing Islamic wares. 168 and 169 are together responsible for the name Ṭarāṭib found in Dussaud 1927: 491 ff. (cf. ibid. map XV).

170a "X". 50 × 30 × 2 m.
P. 1.
b "X".
P, R: Low rise, probably natural: no pottery; mound b is the more notherly.

171a TALL HĀDJDJĪ BAḌR. 400 × 290 × 27 m. D.F.
P. 5, 7, 7a, 9.
R. Poidebard 1934 (map) gives "poste romain", but no traces of Roman material were found. See also Dillemann 1962 maps V and XXVI. Davidson and McKerrell 1976 no. 102 ('Hajji Badden').
b "X". Small modern burial ground.
c "X". ca. 80 × 50 × 2 m. V.
P. NOT VISITED.
R. Modern village, lies 40° east of south from the southeast corner of stone structure on top of 171 a. Not visited, name of village unclear.

172a "X". ca. 70 × 50 × 1 m.
P. 14.
b "X". ca. 40 × 30 × 1 m.
P. 14.
R. Lies west south west of 172 a.

173a al WAṬWAṬĪYA. ca. 50 × 30 × 5 m. V.
P. 12.

173b "X". ca. 80 × 40 × 1 m. C.
P. 14.
R. Relatively modern cemetery; lies southwest of 173 a.

174a "X". ca. 80 × 60 × 2 m.
P. —.
R. Track runs across top. Neither pottery nor flint found, but rise does contain mud brick remains.

b "X". ca. 90 × 60 × 2 m.
P. 12, 13.
R. Located just north of 174 a.

175a TALL ABŪ DHUWĪL. 200 × 100 × 11 m. V.
P. 6, 7, 7a.
R. Elongated mound in C-shape; slopes down from eastern summit. See also Dillemann 1962 maps V and XXVI "T. Abu Dzouil". Although on the latter (= Poidebard's map) it is called "tell important" in the context of the Roman Limes, no traces of the Romans were found here; but see 175 b. Davidson and McKerrell 1976 no. 11.

b "X". ca. 80 × 50 × 9 m.
P. 13.
R. Lies south east of 175 a, across the Wadi. Flint blade. (Perhaps = Davidson and McKerrell 1976 no. 12?).

176 "X". ca. 50 × 50 × 3 m.
P. 8.
R. Partly natural.

177 "X".
P. 13, 14.
R. Three small rises, very few sherds.

178 "X". ca. 250 × 200 × 6 m.
P. 9.
R. Saddle mound. Entirely plowed.

179 TALL SHŪRAQ. 150 × 100 × 35(!) m.
P. 9, 9a.
R. Height measured from stone foundations in Wadi north-northeast of mound. Covered with hard moss. Probably = Dillemann's (map V and p. 80 n. 3) Tcholek.

180 "X". ca. 70 × 50 × 2 m. V.
P. 14.

181 TALL DHIBĀNA. ca 100 × 70 × 1 m. V.
P. 15.

182 al DŪSHA. ca. 100 × 75 × 5 m. V.
P. 9.
R. A black limestone cylinder seal of Late Old Babylonian style was shown by one of the village women, and said to have been found on the mound. It showed an introduction scene w. seated deity, moon crescent, mortal with kid(?), intermediary deity, and as fillers a long haired goat and a dog(?). No illustration available.

183 "X". ca. 40 × 30 × 2 m.
P. 3, 12.
R. Two obsidian fragments.

184 TALL al THŪM. ca. 100 × 100 × 9 m. V.
P. 9, 14a.

185 TALL ḤARB. ca. 100 × 80 × 2 m. V.
P. Too densely inhabited for sherd collecting.

186a TALL ABŪ DJILĀL. ca. 150 × 150 × 5 m.
P. 14.

b "X". ca. 50 × 40 × 5 m. C.
P. 10.
R. Lies west of 186 a. Now used as cemetery for villagers of 186 a.

187a "X". ca. 60 × 50 × 1 m. C.
P. 14.
R. Contains modern burial covered with limestone slabs.

b "X". ca. 80 × 50 × 5 m.
P. 11.
R. Lies ca. 500 m. north west of 187a.

188 TALL ʿAWDA ḤARB. ca. 100 × 100 × 6 m. V.
P. 2, 3.
R. Damaged by *libn* mining.

189 UMM al DJAFĀR FAWQĀNĪ. ca. 100 × 100 × 5 m. V.
P. 14.

190 KHIRBAT KHAZNA. ca. 80 × 50 × 5 m. V.
P. 2, 4.

191 BUWAYRA. ca. 100 × 90 × 3 m. V.
P. Too densely inhabited for sherd collecting.
R. According to one of the policemen in the police station Abū Quṣayyib (no. 196 b) a stone statue was found in this village, presumably similar to the class mentioned under Bayandūr (no. 6). The 1945 map incorrectly gives "Ibn Kālū".

192 "X". ca. 60 × 50 × 15 m. (!).
P. 2, 3, 9, 9a.

193 TALL ṬUWAYYIL. ca. 150 × 100 × 7 m. V.
P. 9, 11.

194 "X". ca. 80 × 60 × 4 m.
P. 8.
R. Now entirely cultivated.

195 TALL GHAZZĀN. 150 × 100 × 12 m. V.
P. 7, 8, 9, 11.
R. Name on map Ghazzāl. Present road (asphalt) runs ca. 1.5 km. east of track indicated on map, cf. section 4.1.

196a "X". ca. 80 × 60 × 5 m. V.
P. 9, 9a.
R. South of asphalt road; sometimes called by same name as no. 196 b.

196b ABŪ QUṢAYYIB. ca. 60 × 50 × 12 m. V.
P. 9.
R. Police station on top.

197 "X". ca. 60 × 50 × 2 m.
P. 1, 2, 4.
R. Now entirely cultivated.

198 MASʿUDA. diam. ca. 300 m. F.V.
P. 14, 15.
R. Ruined modern village spread over three low hillocks.

199 "X". ca. 80 × 70 × 2 m.
P. 9.

200 ḤADJDJĪYA KABĪRA. ca. 80 × 60 × 2 m. V.
P. 14.

201 ḤADJDJĪYA ṢAGHĪRA. ca. 200 × 100 × 4 m. V.
P. 9, 9a.
R. Larger than Ḥ. Habīra!

202 TALL ʿAMARĪN. ca. 130 × 70 × 12 m. F.
P. 7, 8, 9, 14.
R. Slags; basalt bowl.

203a ḤADJDJĪ KABĪR. ca. 60 × 60 × 2 m. V.
P. 9.

b "X". ca. 50 × 50 × 1 m.
P. None.
R. Located due east of a; no sherds, no flint etc.

c "X". ca. 100 × 80 × 2 m. V.
P. 9.
R. Located some 1000 m. SSE of b; also called Ḥadjdjī Kabīr.

204 MUTĪNĪYA. ca. 100 × 100 × 13 m. V.
P. 8, 9, 13, 14.

205 TALL SHARĪSI. ca. 1400 × 700 × 21 m. (!). D.F.C. See fig. 3 and 6a.
P. 7, 8, 9, 9a, 10, 13.
R. From far away this mound looks natural, but it is covered with sherds; it consists of several rises, the highest of which has a small modern cemetery. On the available evidence, identification with *Šeriš* seems not well possible (for Šeriš, cf. Kessler 1980: 137 n. 474; for *Šerši* cf. Hallo 1978: 72). Indicated on map, but I found no mention of Sharīsi in the archaeological literature. The outskirts consist of low, small hillocks, and may represent a city wall.

206 TALL AḤMAD. ca. 100 × 60 × 14 m. V.
P. 7a, 9.

207 TALL ʿANBAR. ca. 80 × 80 × 13 m.
P. 2, 3, 9, 9a, 13, 14.

208a "X". ca. 60 × 60 × 4 m.
P. 14.

b "X". ca. 30 × 30 × 2 m.
P. 9.
R. Due west of a.

209 "X". ca. 40 × 40 × 6 m.
P. 9.
R. Tumulus-like.

210 TALL FARFARA. 1250 × 850 × 27 m. D.F.V.C. See fig. 6b.
P. 4, 6-11.
R. North side fairly straight and steep, south side has separate summit at eastern end. Mentioned but not visited by Poidebard (1934: 163); cf. van Liere 1955: 137; Hrouda 1958: 25; Dillemann 1962: 166 and map VIII. Perhaps remains of a tower at SSW end?

211 "X". ca. 50 × 40 × 3 m.
P. 9.

212 TALL ABŪ TUWAYNA. ca. 100 × 60 × 8 m. V.
P. 7, 8, 9.

213 "X".
P., R. Not visited.

214a "X". ca. 80 × 40 × 2 m. V.
P. 14, 15.
R. Two modern buildings.

b "X". Low rise with modern farm. Not visited. Across road from a.

215a "X". ca. 60 × 50 × 2 m. C.
P. 11.

b "X". diam. ca. 30 m.
P., R. Very low rise. No finds. Lies due east of a, near road.

216 KHUWAYTLA. ca. 80 × 80 × 4 m. V.
P. 10, 12.

217 FARŪDJA. ca. 150 × 100 × 7 m. V.C.
P. 9, 9a, 13.
R. Lies WSW of village called F. on 1945 map.

218a TALL BIṢṢ ṢAGHĪR. 100 × 80 × 15 m. V.C.
P. 9a.
R. Very small rise, probably containing recent farm, lies to the SW of the village.

b "X". ca. 40 m. diameter.
P. 9.
R. Lies just SE of 218 a.

219 TALL BIṢṢ KABIR. ca. 70 × 50 × 12 m. V.
P. 9, 10.
R. To the SE a very small rise produced the same pottery.

220a "X". ca. 30 × 30 × 2 m.
P. 9.

b "X". ca. 25 m. in diam.
P. 9.
R. Lies just both south of 220 a; both lie between main track (leading to Tall Brāk, no. 157) and a northern parallel track.

c "X". ca. 80 × 80 × 3 m.
P. 9, 10.
R. Lies north of parrallel track (cf. b.).

221a KHARĀB al DARĪSIĀT.
P. 9, 13.
R. Kh. al D. is the name of a modern hamlet; to the east lie twin mounds, each ca. 70 × 60 × 10 m.

b "X". ca. 100 × 80 × 2 m. C.
P. 9, 14.
R. Lies ca. 500 m. north of 221 a; consists of three low rises.

222 DARĪSIĀT al KABĪR. ca. 100 × 100 × 18 m.
P. 10.

223 ṬAMNA al BARRĪYA. ca. 50 × 50 × 8 m. V.
P. 14.

224a RAḤĀYA al ṢAWDA. ca. 60 × 60 × 10 m. C.
P. 2, 3.
R. Located ca. 400 m. south of village of same name; not to be confused with b.

b (same). ca. 40 × 40 × 7 m.
P. 9.
R. Located just north of village (cf. a).

225 ḤADDĀDĪYA. V.
P., R. NOT VISITED.

226 "X". ca. 100 × 60 × 4 m.
P. 9.

227 TALL ṬAYYIB. ca. 70 × 60 × 8 m.
P. 10.
R. Few sherds, mound covered with hard moss.

228 TALL ṬAWĀRIDJ. ca. 80 × 50 × 6 m.
P. 9.

229 TALL ṬAWĀRIDJ FAWQĀNI. ca. 50 × 50 × 2 m. V.
P. 9, 9a.

230 "X". ca. 50 × 50 × 2 m.
P. 5a, 9, 13.
R. Now entirely cultivated.

231a TALL MUḤAMMAD ṢAGHĪR. ca. 150 × 100 × 25 m. C.
P. 9, 10, 11.
R. See b. Davidson and McKerrell 1976 No. 103.

b TALL MUḤAMMAD KABĪR. 400 × 300 × 35 m. D.F.
P. 2, 3, 4, 5, 5a, 7, 7a, 8, 9, 9a, 12.
R. Pottery sherd with cylinder seal impression (fig. 9). Both a and b are mentioned, but not discussed, by Poidebard 1934: 140, 147; cf. Dillemann 1962 map V.

c "X". ca. 90 × 50 × 3 m.
P. 8.
R. Located ca. 300 m. north of a.

232 KĪTA. ca. 70 × 50 × 7 m. V.
P. 14.

233 "X". ca. 60 × 50 × 9 m.
P. 9.

234a "X".
P. 7.

b "X". ca. 40 × 40 × 2 m.
P. 10.
R. Located SE of a.

235 ḤABĀRA ṢAGHĪRA / RAZĀZA. ca. 50 × 50 × 3 m. V.
P. 2, 3, 9.

236 "X". ca. 40 × 40 × 3 m.
P. 9, 11, 13.
R. Partly dug away.

237 KHIRBAT DJAMŪ. ca. 100 × 100 × 9 m. V.
P. 2, 9, 9a.

238 "X". ca. 40 × 40 × 2 m.
P. 9.

239 TALL al TIBN. ca. 90 × 60 × 9 m.
P. 2, 6, 7, 9.

240 ḤABĀRA KABĪRA. ca 100 × 80 × 6 m. V.
P. 14.

241 TALL IBRAHĪM al MAḤMŪD. ca. 80 × 60 × 12 m.
P. 9.

242a ʿAMMĀR ṢAGHĪR. ca. 50 × 50 × 9 m.
P. 9.

b MAZRAʿAT TUWAYYIM. ca. 40 × 30 × 2 m.
P. 2, 3, 4, 8.

243a "X". ca. 50 × 40 × 1 m. V.
P. 6, 7.
R. Located due south of no. 231 b. Plowed.

b "X". ca. 70 × 50 × 6 m.
P. 8, 9.
R. Lies slightly north of a, on the edge of the wadi.

244 "X". ca. 80 × 60 × 2 m.
P. 13, 14.

245 TALL DHAHAB. ca. 150 × 80 × 10 m. V.
P. 2, 4, 9, 12, 13.
R. Cf. Dillemann 1962 map V. Davidson and McKerrell 1976 no. 104?

246 TĀQĪT. ca. 170 × 80 × 10 m. F.
P. 7, 7a, 9, 9a.
R. Main and highest mound is ca. 100 m. in length, southern low extension ca. 70 m. Lies beside village Khirbat T.

247 "X".
P., R. NOT VISITED.

248 TALL al ṢATĪḤ. ca. 80 × 60 × 3 m.
P. 14.

249 "X".
P., R. NOT VISITED.

250 TALL SHAMS. ca. 150 × 100 × 9 m. F.V.C.
P. 9.

251 TALL ḤUMAYDĪ. 850 × 550 × 45 m. D.F. See fig. 6c.
P. 7, 7a, 8, 9, 9a, 10.
R. Much baked brick; basalt mortar fragments; about halfway up, the mound shows extensive traces of burning; very faint traces of a moat (cf. van Liere 1963, drawing). See a.o. Poidebard 1934: 147 and pl. 131; van Liere 1963: 114 and drawing. Cf. 278.

252 BŪWĀʻA. ca. 80 × 60 × 2 m. V.
P. 14.

253 KHUWAYTLA. ca. 60 × 60 × 6 m. V.
P. 9.

254 MASHRĪFA ṢAGHĪRA. ca. 150 × 150 × 6 m. V.
P. 14.

255 MASHRĪFA KABĪRA. 200 × 150 × 5 m. V.
P. 9.

256 ṢĀLIḤĪYA. ca. 100 × 100 × 4 m. V.
P. 14.
R. A low rise to the NNW contains the modern village's burials.

257 "X". ca. 80 × 80 × **8** m. C.
P. 9.
R. Just to the east a very small rise contained no pottery.

258 TALL ḤĀMIS. ca. 150 × 100 × 7 m. V.
P. 9, 9a.

259 "X". ca. 40 × 40 × 2 m.
P. 9, 9a.

260 KHIRBAT al SĀDA. ca. 50 × 40 × 2 m. C.
P. 14, 15.
R. Cemetery of modern village al Sāda.

261 TALL MASTĪ ca. 80 × 70 × 8 m. C.
P. 2, 3, 7, 9.

262 TALL ʻADJĪN. ca. 80 × 70 × 3 m.
P. 9, 10.
R. On the 1945 map this site is placed ca. 1 cm. (= 2 km.) too far to the east: from the summit, Tall Barda lies at S 56° E; Barda is located correctly on 1945 map, south of track leading to Brāk.

263 TALL B'IR al ḤIṢĀN. ca. 100 × 80 × 9 m.
P. 9, 11, 13, 14.

264 TALL al SHAʿĪR. ca. 100 × 80 × 4 m.
P. 13, 14.

265 TALL ABŪ ḤUDJAYRA. ca. 80 × 80 × 8 m.
P. 9.

266 KHIRBAT TAFL. ca. 100 × 80 × 3 m. V.
P. 9, 11, 14.

267 TUFFĀḤĪYA. ca. 90 × 80 × 3 m. V.
P. 9, 9a.

268 "X". ca. 60 × 60 × 5 m. C.
P. 4, 10.

269a TALL al DHĪBA. ca. 100 × 80 × 3 m. V.
P. 14.

b SAMĪHA. ca. 100 × 70 × 2 m. V.
P. 14.

270 AL FADʿŪS. ca. 70 × 50 × 2 m. V.
P. 9, 14.

271 "X". ca. 90 × 80 × 2 m.
P. 9.
R. Deserted pump house adjacent to mound.

272 MAṢĪLA. ca. 100 × 100 × 5 m. V.
P. 14.

273a ʿABD ASSAD. ca. 80 × 80 × 2 m.
P. 2, 3, 8.

b "X". ca. 100 × 80 × 4 m.
P. 2, 4, 9.
R. Located NNE of 273a; entirely plowed.

c "X". ca. 70 × 70 × 3 m. C.
P. 2, 9.
R. Located NNW of a.

274 TALL BUṬAYSHA. ca. 70 × 50 × 2 m. V.
P. 9.

275 NIDJMŪK. ca. 100 × 80 × 6 m.
P. 9, 14.

276 TALL QAZZĀL. ca. 100 × 90 × 5 m.
P. 9, 12, 14.

277 TALL ABŪ NADJŪR. 190 × 110 × 12 m.
P. 5a, 7, 8, 9, 9a.

R. Erosion gulley on west side produced crescent-shaped mound. Two buildings. Site is placed 8 mm. (= 1600 m.) too far to the east on the 1945 map.

278 ḤUMAYDĪ. ca. 100 × 100 × 6 m. V.
P. 14, 15.
R. Village belonging to, and bearing same name as the large mound (no. 251).

279 "X". ca. 60 × 40 × 2 m.
P. 9, 14.

280 "X". ca. 100 × 90 × 2 m. C.
P. 14.
R. Almost entirely plowed.

281 "X". ca. 60 × 40 × 1 m.
P. 8.
R. Entirely plowed.

282 TALL SHAYKH NIMS. 240 × 120 × 18 m. D.F.C.
P. 1, 4-9.
R. See Poidebard 1934: 147 and pl. 130[1] ("Namès"): "Enceinte invisible du sol". Also Dillemann 1962: 200 (= map XXVI) "tell incorpé dans le limes". No Roman period material was found by us.

283 UMM KĪF. 230 × 100 × 12 m. F.
P. 7, 7a, 9, 9a, 12.

284 TALL QUSHLA. ca. 100 × 100 × 15 m.
P. 2, 9, 9a.
R. The 1945 map is incorrect in this area: both Qushla and Maʿaz should be moved north ca 15 mm., Maʿaz (no. 286) also slightly westward.

285a "X". ca. 120 × 100 × 16 m. F.
P. 8, 9, 9a.

b "X". F.
P. 9.
R. Lies on the Djaghdjagh, N 17° W of Maʿaz (no. 286) and S 20° E of no. 285 a.

c "X".
P. Nothing found.
R. Lies across the stream from 285 b, i.e. east of the latter.

286 TALL MAʿAZ. ca. 130 × 100 × 17 m. F.C.
P. 7, 7a, 9, 13.
R. Site should be moved to the NW on the 1945 map (see no. 284).

287 "X". ca. 80 × 60 × 2 m.
P. 14.

288a "X".
P. 7.
b "X".
P. 7 (very few sherds).
R. a and b are the summits of a mound with a 'saddle'.

289 TALL BARRĪ. ca. 500 × 400 × 40 m. F.C.
P. 2, 4, 5a, 7, 7a, 8, 9, 9a, 10, 12, 14.
R. Identified with ancient Kaḫat. For literature see Poidebard 1934 pl. 130[2]; RlA V 3/4: 287 (Postgate); most recently: Pecorella and Salvini 1981/2.

290 "X". ca. 60 × 40 × 2 m.
P. 13.

6.0 *Pottery*. The validity of the results of a survey depend in large measure on the correct dating of the pottery sherds and other artefacts encountered. In this context the permission granted by the Syrian Directorate of Antiquities and Museums to remove a selection of sherds to Amsterdam again deserves grateful mention, as leisurely comparison with a library and a reference collection at hand greatly enhances the credibility of the attributions. I wish to thank also Dr. Giorgio Buccellati, Dr. Hartmut Kühne, Dr. Winfried Orthmann and Dr. Eva Strommenger for the opportunity to view and discuss the pottery produced by their excavations.

6.1. Nevertheless, difficulties abounded, both of a theoretical and of a practical nature. First, the area under consideration is not well known from stratigraphic excavation. Tall Brāk, Tall Barrī and Tall Laylān have to all practical purposes as yet only been sounded superficially, and completed—and completely published—excavations outside the area (e.g., Ḥamā, the lake Assad region, K͟huwayra, Fuk͟h-k͟hārīya, Nineveh and the ʿAmuq) have as a disadvantage the very fact that they are far removed, and comparison with them may thus obscure differences in regional development. Second, some aspects of the appearance of the sherds were—for want of a technical analysis—described in a subjective fashion; this is compounded by the failure in some publication to describe pottery characteristics other than shape at all, thus greatly reducing the validity of comparisons.

6.2 The sherds illustrated in this article have been chosen either because they serve as prototypes and are datable, or because no close parallel could be found, and their dating therefore was unclear to the writer. Obviously, of the ca. 40.000 sherds handled in the course of the survey, a sample of less than 200 cannot give a picture of the full range of types encountered. I have nevertheless tried to make this sample as representative as possible, illustrating both known (figs. 12-25) and unknown types (figs. 26-27). Some of the latter may eventually prove to belong to the periods that are now less well documented, such as the Late Bronze and Iron Age.

6.3 The illustrations are arranged roughly chronologically; for the absolute dates of the following categories, cf. the table in fig. 11. The categories have been coded as follows:

1	Pre-Ḥalaf, Amuq A and B		fig. 12
2	Ḥalaf, Amuq C and D		fig. 13
3	Ubaid, Amuq E		fig. 14
4	Uruk and other late 4th millennium BC (Amuq F)		fig. 15, 16
5	EB I	5a Nineveh 5 [14]	fig. 17

[14] Recent findings (e.g. communications by H. Weiss and by J. Moon-Killick at the XXX Rencontre Assyriologique Internationale, Leiden 1983) suggest that *Nineveh 5* can occur together with Late Uruk beveled rim bowls (cf. also Fielden 1981: 159), but as it continues far into the third millennium, it is here grouped with EB I. Also the Amuq G 'Incised and Impressed Ware' (OIP 61: 277 ff.) is classified under this heading.

6	EB II		fig. 18 a-d
7	EB III	7a 'Metallische Ware'	fig. 18 e-r
8	EB IV		fig. 19
9	MB	9a 'Khabūr Ware'	fig. 20-24 f
10	LB		fig. 24 g-k
11	Iron Age		fig. 25 a-f
12	Hellenistic, Roman, Parthian		fig. 25 g-j, 17 l-n
13	Byzantine		
14	'Islamic' [15]		fig. 25 k, l

6.3.1 These categories conform to the periodization now in the process of being proposed for Syria (cf. Mardikh pp. 60 and 115). Nevertheless, dating individual unstratified sherds is in many cases still somewhat problematic. In the course of this survey, little 'Red and Black Burnished' were has been found (i.e. the Khirbat Kerak- and Transcaucasian-related ware, Amuq H and I), Tall Farfara (no. 210) providing a notable exception. Lacking such distinctive wares as the Red and Black Burnished, or Multiple Brush Painted (Amuq G-H), the distinctions made here between Early Bronze I, II and III should be seen as tentative. EB I-II (Amuq G-H) were here mainly characterized by shapes in 'Plain Simple Ware' (cf. OIP 61: 264 ff).

6.3.2 Another example of the problems involved in dating pottery is the attribution of the ware variously known as *Akkadian Ware*, *Metallische Ware* or *Grey Ware* (cf. Kühne 1976, together with P. Spanos, Zeitschrift für Assyriologie 67 1977: 289-298, esp. pp. 292-295). In the present report, this ware has been classed in "7a", the EB III period, although it continues into, and occurs often in, the EB IV period. As in the preceding case, the limits of these categories should be considered flexible (a consequence of moving category *7a* to *8* would be a more gradual upward slope of the graph in fig. 6).
No subdivisions have been made in either the MB or LB. This might be done in an excavation on the basis of parallels in other classes of artefacts, but for most pottery shapes, developments within these periods in Syria are too gradual to warrant such subdivisions.

6.3.3 Another notable problem is our lack of information regarding ceramics of the Iron Age, resulting in doubtful validity of fig. 6 in that respect [16].

[15] Only indicated where a considerable presence was noted; most mounds have some glazed or other Islamic ware on the surface.

[16] Some shapes from Nimrud are treated in Lines 1954 and Oates 1959; M. Lebeau's La Ceramique de l'Age du Fer II-III à tell Abu Danné (Paris 1983) became available only after completion of this manuscript; thus only a few parallels could be incorporated.

6.3.4 In the following catalogue, the entries are accompanied by a few observations on the appearance of the sherds. No clay analyses were attempted, and the observations are therefore 'macroscopic' and to some degree subjective. The order in the description is:

Manufacture:	*hand- or wheelmade* [17]
Temper:	without proper analysis, verdicts under this heading are at best tentative, but it is believed that the indications given are useful pointers for further study. "No vis.t." means *no visible temper*.
Paste:	a rough division is made here between coarse, medium and fine: as a rule of thumb, regularly occuring interruptions of the surface of a break (inclusions, airbubbles etc.) larger than ca. 0.5 mm. were taken to indicate coarseness. If the break presented a 'closed' surface (either flat or jagged) to the eye, the verdict was 'fine'. No attempt has been made to distinguish between "high-" or "low fired", unless sherds were very soft, or vitrified. the great majority of the encountered sherds were baked to a hard touch and sound.
Colour of the paste:	no use was made of a Munsell Colour Chart.
Site:	The number of the site where the sherd was found is given, followed by a note concerning possible parallels, if applicable.

6.3.5 NB: It should be noted that, whereas presence of wares recognized in the field was based on body- and feature-sherds, the illustrations only present a selection of the latter (i.e., rims, bases and decorated sherds). Roman 'Red Pergame Ware' is easily noticed in the field, as are Byzantine roof tiles; their presence was duly noted, but no examples were collected or illustrated, as of the former only bodysherds were seen and the latter were too bulky for transport. The attribution of sites to the EB III and IV periods is often based on the frequent occurrence of fragments of the well-known goblets. Only a small selection of these was collected (cf. fig. 19n).

6.4 *Catalogue of illustrated sherds.*

fig. 12 *Pre-Halaf (code 1)*

a. Handmade. (coiled?). Chaff + lime. Rough exterior. Coarse paste, orange, black core. *197*. Amuq B/C Dark Faced Unburnished Ware.
b. Handmade. Chaff. + grit or 'quartz'. Coarse paste, orange walls, black core. Outside burnished, + inside rim. Low firing. *197*. Amuq A-C DFB.

[17] Following the principle of OIP 61: 232 n. 9, no distinction is made as to the fastness of the wheel.

c. Handmade. Bottom edge frgm. of 'husking tray'. Chaff. + large grits. Rough exterior. Coarse black paste. *197*. Cf. Hassuna II-IV, JNES IV 1945: fig. 3:10.
d. Handmade. Lime. Med. paste, cream. *96*. Amuq B Coarse Simple Ware.
e. Handmade. Chaff + lime. Fine paste, orange exterior. *63*. Cf. Amuq B Coarse Simple Ware (OIP 61:70).
f. Handmade. Chaff. Fine paste. Buff walls, black core. *242*[b]. Amuq A-C DFB (cf. OIP 61: fig. 47).
g. Handmade. Chaff. Med-fine paste, black core, buff walls. *282*. Amuq A-B Coarse Simple Ware (OIP 61, fig. 41:45.
h. Handmade. Chaff + fine grit. Med. coarse paste, blackish core. Brown, burnished in- and outside. *106*. Amuq A-C DFB, cf. OIP 61, fig. 22:18-20, or fig. 107:3.

fig. 13 *Halaf etc. (code 2)*

a. Handmade. Lime. Smoothed. Med. paste, cream (dark core). *63*. Amuq C Dark Faced Unburnished Ware, cf. OIP 61: 141 ff, and fig. 111:4.
b. Handmade. No vis. t. Fine paste, cream-light green. *242*[b]. Amuq C DF Unburnished Ware (OIP 61: 141f.).
c. Handmade. Chaff + lime. Med. paste, orange walls, blackish core. Smoothed surfaces. *190*. Amuq D Wiped-burnish Ware (OIP 61:160ff.).
d. Handmade. Sand-t. Fine paste, orange throughout. Thin dark-red-brown paint on out- and inside, partly worn off. *106*. Cf. Iraq II 1935 fig. 64:3, 4, 5.
e. Handmade. Chaff. Med. paste, buff, cream wash, dark paint. *125*.
f. Handmade. Chaff + grit. Coarse paste, buff walls, grey/black core. Inside burnished. *231*[b]. Amuq 'First Mixed Range'; OIP 61 fig. 79:4.
g. Handmade. Lime + sand. Fine paste, orange throughout. Burnished exterior. Blackish lustrous paint. *7*. Cf. OIP 61 fig. 87:25 or 115:21.
h. Handmade. Sand + grit + lime. Fine paste, buff. Orange buff paint. *7*. Cf. OIP 61 fig. 116:14, or fig. 87:10.
i. Handmade(?). Sand. Fine paste, orange buff. Buff wash, brown paint. *7*. Although the design of the hatched diabolo is reminiscent of the Ubaid period (cf. Tobler 1950 pl. 137 no. 284) its combination with filled diabolo's is unique; the ware looks more like Halaf.

fig. 14 *Ubaid etc. (code 3)*

a. Handmade. Chaff + grit. Med. paste, black core with orange walls. *282*. Amuq E 'New Style Cooking Pot Ware' (OIP 61: fig. 139:3).
b. Handmade. Fine chaff + lime(?). Fine paste. Some burnish over the dark brown paint and cream background. *63*. Amuq E.
c. Handmade(?). Chaff. Med-fine paste, black core, orange/buff walls. *53*. Amuq E 'New Cooking Pot Ware', cf. OIP 61: fig. 139:3-9.
d. Handmade. Chaff + lime. Med-coarse paste, cream. *96*. Cf. Amuq E Simple Ware (OIP 61 fig. 142:26, 27).

e. Handmade. Fine chaff + lime(?). Med. paste, black core, cream walls. *96*. Amuq E Simple Ware.
f. Wheelmade?. Plant + lime. Med. paste, grey core. Cream wash, light brown paint. *96*. Cf. OIP 61 fig. 144:8.
g. Handmade. Lime. Med. paste, greyish core, cream outside ('sandwich'). *88*. Amuq E Simple Ware (OIP 61 fig. 146:17).
h. Handmade. Lime. Fine paste. Buff. Smoothed exterior. *242*[b]. Typical of Southern Ubaid, cf. Iraq XXII pl. XIIIa. (Eridu XIV-XII).
i. Handmade. Fine chaff + lime. Med. paste, cream. Dark brown paint. *63*. For design cf. OIP 61 fig. 148:6.
j. Wheelmade. Sand. Fine paste, buff. Dark paint. *231*[b]. Cf. Tobler 1950 nos. 243-245.
k. Handmade. No vis. t. Fine paste, greenish. Brown paint. *242*[b]. Somewhat like Tobler 1950 nos. 208, 240.
l. Handmade. Lime. Fine paste, buff. Brown paint. *242*[b]. Shape, cf. OIP 61 fig. 150:27-32.
m. Wheelmade. Chaff + lime. Med-fine paste. Cream. Brown paint. *146*. Somewhat like OIP 61 fig. 149:36.
n. Handmade. No vis. t. Cream. Red-brown paint. *245*. Amuq E cf. OIP 61 fig. 152:3, 12, 13.

fig. 15 *Uruk etc. (code 4)*

a. Wheelmade. Sand. Med-fine paste. Dark core, buff walls. Lustrous brown paint. *146*. Amuq F Simple Ware, cf. OIP 61 fig. 171:4, 5 (painted).
b. Wheelmade. Lime. Med-fine paste, buff with greyish core. Paint on rim reddish and lustrous. *82*. Amuq F see above.
c. Wheelmade. Chaff + lime. Fine paste, dark core, buff walls. Dark brown paint outside. *53*. Amuq F cf. OIP 61 fig. 171:7.
d. Wheelmade(?). Chaff. Med-fine paste, buffish grey. *273*[b]. Amuq F cf. OIP 61 fig. 171:4.
e. Wheelmade. No vis. t. Fine paste, grey-green. *53*. cf. Tobler 1950: no. 384.
f. Handmade(?). Lime. Med-fine paste, buff. *210*. Amuq F cf. OIP 61 fig. 171:7.
g. Handmade. Chaff. Coarse paste, orange-cream. Coarse exterior, wheathered. *106*. Amuq F Chaff-f. Simple Ware, cf. OIP 61 fig. 176:3.
h. Wheelmade. Fine lime. Fine paste, buff. *231*[b]. Amuq F Smooth-Faced Simple Ware (OIP 61 fig. 171:10-17).
i. Wheelmade(?). Lime. Fine paste, orange buff. *126*. Amuq F. Smooth Faced Simple Ware, cf. OIP 61 fig. 171:18.
j. Wheelmade. Lime. Fine paste, buff. *53*. See above.
k. Handmade. Sand. Med-fine paste, grey. Outside burnished orange. *88*. Like (unpublished) Ḥammām al Turkmān (north of Raqqa) Late-Chacolithic.

l. Handmade. Chaff -t. Coarse paste, black core, brown walls. Burnished. *71*. Amuq F Chaff-f. Simple Ware, with shape more like OIP 61 fig. 179:20.

fig. 16 (*Uruk etc. cont'd*)

a. Wheelmade(?). Chaff + lime. Med. paste, black core, buff walls, some burnish. *71*. Amuq F (OIP 61 fig. 176).
b. Handmade. Fine chaff. Fine paste, buff-cream. *175*. Amuq F Chaff-f. Simple Ware, cf. OIP 61 fig. 176.
c. Handmade. Chaff. Coarse paste, black w. cream walls. *242^b*. Chaff-faced Simple Ware, cf. OIP 61 fig. 176:27.
d. Handmade. Coarse sand in fine paste, orange. *282*. Amuq F cf. OIP 61 fig. 176 and p. 237-8 ('various clays').
e. Wheelmade. Sand. Med-fine paste, occasional large pebbly inclusions; greyish core, buff-orange walls. *242^b*. Cf. Tobler 1950 f. 442, but larger.
f. Handmade. Chaff + lime. Rough exterior. Coarse paste, orange, black core. *197*. Amuq F Chaff-faced Simple Ware. (OIP 61 fig. 176).
g. Wheelmade. Lime. Med-fine paste, cream. *92*. Cf. Sürenhagen 1978 Tab. 24:41.
h. Wheelmade. Sand. Med. paste, buff w. greyish core. Incised hatched triangles on shoulder. *11*. Cf., e.g., Sürenhagen 1978 Tab. 37, 38.
i. Handmade(?). Lime. Med. paste with darkish core, orange walls. *25*. Somewhat similar to Delougaz 1952 pl. 64:18.
j. Wheelmade. Cheff + lime. Med-fine paste, black core, buff walls. *242^b*. Cf. Tobler 1950 fig. 405-7.

fig. 17 (*EB I code 5*))

a. Wheelmade. . Lime Med-fine paste, buff. Creamy 'wash', not ubiquitous due to diff. firing. *96*. Amuq G Plain Simple Ware, cf. OIP 61 fig. 205:9, 10.
b. Handmade. Grit. Med. paste, buff. *82*. Amuq G, prob. 'Third Cooking Pot Ware', cf. OIP 61 fig. 290f.
c. Wheelmade. Fine lime. Fine paste, cream. *210*. Amuq G, OIP 61 fig. 210:3, 13.
d. Wheelmade. No vis. t. Fine paste, buff. *282*. Amuq Plain Simple Ware (OIP 61 fig. 209:2, 3).
e. Wheelmade. Chaff. Med-fine paste, buff walls, grey core. *163*. Amuq G cf. OIP 61 fig. 207:2.
f. Wheelmade. No vis. t. Very fine paste, grey. Vertical burnish. *175*. Amuq G, cf. OIP 61 fig. 217:3.
g. Wheelmade. Lime. Fine paste, buff grey-greenish (mainly green outside, due to high firing). *231^b*. Amuq G Plain Simple Ware, cf. OIP 51 fig. 211:2.
h. Wheelmade. No vis. t. Fine paste, grey core, buff walls. *53*. Amuq G Plain Simple Ware, OIP 61 fig. 211:6.

Nineveh V (code 5^a)

i. Wheelmade. No vis. t. Fine paste, cream. Incised. *231^t*. Amuq G 'Incised and Impressed Ware', cf. OIP 61 fig. 221:12, 13.

j. Wheelmade. Fine lime. Fine paste, cream. Very light incisions (before firing) under rim, clearer on belly of vessel. *231^{b}*. Shape like OIP 61 fig. 221:15; for light incisions, ibid. p. 281.

k. Wheelmade(?). Prob. lime. Fine paste, cream. *277*. Nineveh V. No exact parallel for design found, but ware is same as above.

l, m and n: see under code 12: Hell., Rom., Parthian

o. Wheelmade. No vis. t. Fine paste, green buff. *106*. Impressions somewhat like LAAA XX 1933 pl. LXII:12; cf. ibid. XIX pl. LX:6.

fig. 18 *EB II (code 6)*

a. Wheelmade. No vis. t. Fine paste, cream. High firing resulted in greenish colour on outisde and over rim. *210*. Amuq G Plain Simple Ware (OIP 61 fig. 206:4-6).

b. Wheelmade. No vis. t. Fine paste. Buff-grey. *82*. Amuq G Plain Simple Ware. Cf. above.

c. Wheelmade. Sand-t. Fine paste, green through high firing. *231^{b}*. Amuq G Plain Simple Ware. Cf. also E. Speiser, Excavations at Tepe Gawra I (Philadelphia 1935) no. 22.

d. Handmade. Chaff. Med. paste, grey core, mottled brown-red burnished. *210*. Somewhat like E. Speiser, Excavations at Tepe Gawra I (Philadelphia 1935) no. 20, from Gawra VIII B. Probably import from Anatolia. On Red and Black Burnished Ware, see infra 6.3.1.

EB III (code 7)

e. Wheelmade. Sand. Med-fine paste, grey core, orange walls. Burnished outside and just over rim. *231^{b}*. Cf. Halawa Tf. 57:6.

f. Wheelmade. No vis. t. Fine paste, buff. Rim turned off nonchalantly. *282*. Cf. Kühne 1976 Abb. 169.

g. Wheelmade. Grit + sand. Med-coarse paste, dark core, buff walls. *106*.

h. Wheelmade. No vis. t. Very fine paste, cream. *282*. Cf. Halawa Tf. 55:19.

i. Wheelmade. Grit + sand. Med-fine paste, grey. Some burnish. *134*.

j. Wheelmade. Chaff + lime(?). Very fine paste (almost 'vitrified'), grey core, orange-buff walls. *289*. Cf. Kühne 1976: Abb. 40.

k. Wheelmade. No vis. t. Fine paste, cream. *175*. Cf. Halawa Tf. 55:18.

l. Wheelmade. Fine paste, cream. *14*. Cf. Halawa Tf. 58:13.

m. Wheelmade. Lime. Fine paste, buff-green. *134*. Cf. Delougaz 1952 pl. 146, 147.

n. Handmade? Coarse sand in fine paste, orange. *282*. Cf. Kühne 1976 Abb. 184?

Metallische Ware (code 7^{a})

o. Wheelmade. No vis. t. Fine paste, grey. Burnished. *289*. For shape cf. Kühne 1976 Abb. 22.

p. Wheelmade. No vis. t. Very fine paste (almost vitrified), buff. *106*. (cf. Selenkahiye unpublished).

q. Wheelmade. No vis. t. Very fine paste, grey. Burnish. *53*. Cf. Kühne 1976 Tf. 7:2.
r. Wheelmade. Fine lime? Fine paste, grey-green. Part of stack of at least 9 bowls which sagged in the kiln and melted together. *44*. cf. Kühne 1976: Abb. 84.

fig. 19 *EB IV (code 8)*.
a. Wheelmade. Fine sand(?) + lime(?). Fine paste, greyish core, buff walls. *231*[b]. cf. Hama fig. 103:3D 697.
b. Wheelmade. Lime. Fine paste. Cream. *53*. Cf. Mardikh 98:5 or Halawa Tf. 55:9.
c. Wheelmade. Lime + chaff. Med-fine paste, grey; burnished. Bubbly crack through middle of wall, as if markedly differential pression was applied inside and outside during turning. *125*. Cf. Kühne 1976 Abb. 198.
d. Wheelmade. Lime. Med-fine paste, buff. *98*. Cf. Kühne 1976 Abb. 198.
e. Wheelmade. 'Calcite'. Coarse paste, buff walls, dark grey core. Occasional burnish on rim. *163*. Cf. Mardikh, figure 18, 19.
f. Wheelmade. Lime + chaff. Med-fine paste, buff. *282*. Cf. Mardikh fig. 18, 19.
g. Wheelmade. Grit + lime. med-fine paste, grey core, green outside. *53*. Cf. Mardikh fig. 18, 19.
h. Wheelmade. Chaff. Fine paste, orange walls, blackish core. *282*. This vessel was apparently set to dry, but soon provided with a new coating of clay before the original had dried entirely. Positioning of sherd in drawing may vary slightly. Somewhat like Kühne 1976: Abb. 158.
i. Wheelmade. Lime. Med-fine paste, buff. *53*. Cf. Halawa Tf. 66:79.
j. Wheelmade. Lime + chaff. med-fine paste, buff-cream. *12*. Deep incisions. Cf. Kühne 1976 Tf. 31:5, 6.
k. Wheelmade. Lime. Fine paste, buff/cream. *242*[b]. cf. Amuq Painted Simple Ware? (no paint on outside, but latter is worn). Painted band inside rim. Cf. Halawa Tf. 64:1.
l. Wheelmade. No vis. t. Fine paste, buff. Two-tone brown paint. *71*. Amuq J Painted Simple Ware.
m. Wheelmade. Lime. Fine paste, buff, some red on outside (differential oxidation during firing). *96*. Cf. Hama fig. 58:3G 378.
n. Wheelmade. Fine lime. Fine paste, buff-orange, cream 'wash' here and there turned orange from uneven oxidation during firing. *98*. Amuq J Plain Simple Ware Goblet.

fig. 20 *MB (code 9)*
a. Wheelmade. Lime? + few large grits. Buff; vertical burnish outside. *245*. Cf. Halawa Tf. 43:24, 26.
b. Wheelmade. Chaff + lime. Med-fine paste, cream. *98*. Cf. Dornemann, AASOR 44 fig. 23:12, and 20:43.
c. Wheelmade. Some lime. Fine paste, cream walls, orange core. *82*. Cf. Halawa Tf. 44:1.

d. Wheelmade. Lime + grit + some chaff. Med-fine paste, orange-buff. *171*. Cf. Dornemann, AASOR 44 fig. 22:12.
e. Wheelmade. Lime + chaff. Med. paste, cream. Remains of brown paint on rim and outside, prob. in wide bands, inside surface worn, exposing chaff-imprints. *116*. Cf. Dornemann, AASOR 44 fig. 23:15.
f. Wheelmade. Chaff + grit. Fine paste with some coarse grits, grey core, buff walls. *98*.
g. Wheelmade. Chaff + some lime. Med. paste, buff. *98*.
h. Wheelmade. Chaff + lime. Fine paste, cream. *282*.
i. Wheelmade. Chaff + lime. Med-paste, buff. *98*.
j. Wheelmade. Lime. Med-fine paste, cream. *125*.

fig. 21 (MB cont'd)
a. Wheelmade. Lime + chaff. Fine paste, buff w. grey core. *282*.
b. Wheelmade. Chaff. Med. paste, black core, buff walls. *125*.
c. Coiled(?). Grit. Med-coarse paste, orange/buff. *205*. cf. Dornemann, AASOR 44 fig. 21:30. The illustrations 20 f-j and 21 a-c are all in the MB profiled rim and/or -wall tradition, cf. Halawa TF 45:19-24, Mardikh fig. 36-38, and Dornemann AASOR 44 fig. 21:30-37 and fig. 22:25-34.
d. Wheelmade. Lime. Med-fine paste, buff. *231*[b]. Cf. Mardikh fig. 34:6.
e. Wheelmade. Lime. Fine paste, buff. *282*. Cf. Hama fig. 109:3C 83.
f. Wheelmade. Lime. Fine paste, cream. *282*. Cf. Mardikh fig. 40:5.
g. Wheelmade. No vis. t. Fine paste, grey. *134*. Cf. Mardikh fig. 41:11.
h. Wheelmade. Lime. Med. paste, orange-cream walls, dark core. *231*[a]. Cf. Mardikh fig. 40:1 (which is smaller).
i. Wheelmade. Lime + some chaff. Fine paste, cream. *98*.
j. Wheelmade. Fine lime. Fine paste, grey, burnished. *231*[a]. Cf. Mardikh fig. 34:4.
k. Wheelmade. Lime + chaff. Med. paste, grey core, buff walls. *53*. cf. Halawa Tf. 44:6.
l. Wheelmade. Lime + chaff. Med-fine paste, buff. *210*. Somewhat like Halawa Tf. 44:6.
m. Wheelmade. Lime + sand. Med. paste, buff walls, orange core. Paint over rim. *82*. Shape like Hama fig. 127:2D 17. Perhaps in Khabūr tradition.

fig. 22 (*MB cont'd*)
a. Wheelmade. Sand. Med-fine paste, buff; cream 'wash' outside. 'Cuneiform' impressions on upper shoulder. *98*. Shape somewhat like Halawa Tf. 45:24.
b. Wheelmade. Chaff + lime. Med-fine paste, buff, cream wash outside. *282*. Cf. Halawa Tf. 46:2.
c. Wheelmade. Chaff + lime. Med. paste, orange walls, black core. *282*. Cf. Halawa Tf. 46:1.
d. Wheelmade. Lime + sand. Fine paste, buff. *283*. Somewhat like Halawa Tf. 46:15.

e. Wheelmade. Lime. Med-fine paste, orange buff, cream outside. *53*. Cf. Halawa Tf. 46:17.
f. Wheelmade(?). Sand. Med-fine paste, cream. *82*. Somewhat like Halawa Tf. 48:6.
g. Wheelmade. Sand(?). Fine paste, buff; lighter walls (slip?). *171*. Cf. Hama fig. 120:2C 897.
h. Wheelmade. Lime. Fine paste, orange. *53*. Cf. Halawa Tf. 48:6.
i. Wheelmade. Lime. Med-fine paste, green. *134*. Cf. Halawa Tf. 48:8.
j. Wheelmade. Lime + chaff. Med. paste, greenish. *96*. Cf. Halawa Tf. 48:28.

fig. 23 (*MB cont'd*)
a. Wheelmade. Lime + sand. Fine paste, green. *106*. Cf. Halawa Tf. 47:11, 12.
b. Wheelmade. Lime. Fine paste, buff with grey core. *282*. Cf. Halawa Tf. 44:16.
c. Wheelmade. Grit + lime. Med-coarse paste with large inclusions, dark core, buff walls. *53*. Cf. Halawa Tf. 44:10.
d. Wheelmade. No vis. t. Fine paste, orange. *263*. Cf. Halawa Tf. 48:15.
e. Wheelmade. Lime. med-fine paste, buff. *202*. Cf. g.
f. Wheelmade. Sand. med-fine paste, orange, cream slip. *210*. Cf. Halawa Tf. 44:19.
g. Wheelmade. Lime + chaff. Med-fine paste, buff-cream. *205*. Cf. Halawa Tf. 48:26.
h. Wheelmade. Chaff + lime. Med. paste, cream. *282*. Cf. Halawa Tf. 47:14.

Khabūr Ware (code 9a)

i. Wheelmade. Lime. Med-fine paste, buff. *231*[b]. Cf. Mallowan 1936 fig. 17:14.
j. Wheelmade. Fine lime. Fine paste, cream-green outside half, orange inside half, along well-defined dividing line. Dark paint on rim. *98*.
k. Wheelmade. Lime. Med-fine paste, black core, buff walls. Red paint on rim only. *125*. Cf. Speiser, Museum Journal XXIII 1933 pl. LIX:2.
l. Wheelmade. Lime. Fine paste, buff-cream. Red-brown painted bands. 109. Cf. Hrouda 1957: Tf. 8.

fig. 24 (*Khabūr Ware cont'd*)
a. Wheelmade. Chaff + lime. Med-fine paste, grey core, buff walls. Brown paint. *98*. Like Halawa Tf. 45:14; paint in Khabūr tradition.
b. Wheelmade. Lime. Fine paste, cream/green. Dark paint (also on and over rim). *98*. Reminiscent of Mallowan 1936 fig. 16:5.
c. Wheelmade. Lime. Fine paste, buff. Darkbrown paint. *251*. Cf. Mallowan 1937: fig. 21:1.
d. Wheelmade. Lime. Med-fine paste, buff. Dark paint. *231*[b]. Cf. Mallowan 1937 fig. 21:1, 12.
e. Wheelmade. Sand. Fine paste, cream. Brown paint. *231*[b]. Cf. Mallowan 1937 fig. 24:8 and 22:11.
f. Wheelmade. Lime. Fine paste, cream. *134*.

LB (code 10)

g. Wheelmade. Chaff. + lime. Med. paste, grey core, light grey walls. *155*. Cf. R. Starr, Nuzi II (Cambridge, Ma. 1937) pl. 89 P, for shape and ware.

h. Wheelmade. Lime. Fine paste, buff-green. *134*. Cf. Delougaz 1952 pl. 146, 147.

i. Wheelmade. Lime. Med-fine paste, buff. *210*. Cf. Dornemann, AASOR 44, fig. 20:12, 13.

j. Wheelmade. Lime Med-fine paste, orange. *231*[b]. Cf. Dornemann, AASOR 44 Fig. 20:14.

k. Wheelmade. Lime + grit. Med-fine paste with large inclusions, grey core, buff walls. Some burnish. *205*.

fig. 25 *Iron Age (code 11)*

a. Wheelmade. Lime + chaff. Med-fine paste, grey walls w. brown-grey core. *277*. Cf. Lebeau 1983 fig. VII:1.

b. Wheelmade. Lime. Fine paste, orange-cream. *210*. Cf. Fukhkharīya no. 53.

c. Handmade. Grit. Med-fine paste, buff. *72*. Iron Age? cf. Lebeau 1983 fig. XIX BL 15?

d. Wheelmade. Lime. Fine paste, cream, *231*[a]. Cf. Fukhkharīya no. 55.

e. Wheelmade. No vis. t. Fine paste, grey. *98*. Cf. Speiser, Museum Journal XXIII 1933 pl. LXVI:6.

f. Wheelmade. Lime. Med-fine paste, cream; buffish core. *195*. cf. Lines 1954 pl. 38:4.

Hellenistic, Roman, Parthian (code 12)

g. Handmade. Sand. Med. paste, orange buff. Decoration: red paint, impressed triangles, stamped rayed sun-discs. *155*. cf. Hrouda, Tell Halaf IV (Berlin 1962) pl. 85:13, 14.

h. Wheelmade. Lime. Med-fine paste, grey-green core. Smoothed + scraped outside, stamped. *245*.

i. Wheelmade. Line. Fine paste, cream-green (high firing). Blackish paint. *286*. Cf. Hrouda, Tell Halaf IV (Berlin 1962) Tf. 84:3.

j. Wheelmade. Grit. Coarse paste, buff. Rosettes stamped. *72*.

fig. 17(!)

l. Wheelmade. No vis. t. Fine pate, cream. Impressed w. stamp. *289*. Cf. Pecorella and Salvini 1982: 60 abd pl. 7^2.

m. Prob. belonging to some vessel as l. Wheelmade, rest of descr. same. *289*.

n. Wheelmade(?). No vis. t. Very fine paste, orange. Stamped 'dotted' lozenges. Bitumen on inside sherd. *230*. Comparable to l and m.

fig. 25 *'Islamic' (code 14)*

k. Wheelmade. Lime. Fine paste, cream. Impressed decoration. *98*.

l. Wheelmade. Lime. Fine paste, cream-green. *125*.

Fig. 26 *Pieces for which no exact parallels could be found*

a. Wheelmade. Grit + chaff. Med. paste, buff. Red paint on upper outside and just over rim. *205*.

b. Wheelfinished coiled. Chaff. Coarse paste, cream. Circles stamped with reed-end. *231^b*.

c. Wheelmade. Fine lime. Fine paste, orange core, cream walls. Orange 'wash'. Red paint. (vessel probably held in paint upside down; sploshes on outside). *51*

d. Wheelmade. Lime. Med-fine paste. Cream. Finger impressions and deep incisions. *155*.

e. Handmade (coiled up from flat plate). Chaff. Coarse paste, black, w. orange-cream walls. 'Cabled' handle-ridge. *82*.

f. Handmade(??). Chaff + lime. Med-fine paste, grey core, buff walls. *98*.

h. Wheelmade. Lime. Med. paste, buff. *231^b*. Cf. Delougaz 1952: pl. 147?

i. 'Wheelmade'. Coarse lime. Coarse paste, buff throughout. Exterior mottled orange-black due to secondary fire. *98*.

j. Wheelmade. Lime + chaff. Med-fine paste, buff. Red paint. *231^b*.

k. Wheelmade. Chaff. + lime. Fine paste, buff; grey core. *23*.

fig. 27 (*no exact parallels, cont'd*)

a. Wheelmade. Lime. Med. paste. Buff. Brown paint over and just under rim. *146*.

b. Wheelmade. Lime. Fine paste, orange walls, grey-buff interior. *231^b*.

c. Wheelmade. Lime. Fine paste, buff. Paint darkbrown-black. *231^b*.

d. Wheelmade. Lime + chaff. Fine paste, grey-buff. *134*.

e. Wheelmade. Fine sand. Med-fine paste, buff with dark core. Reddish paint. *231^b*. Late Uruk? Cf. perhaps OIP 61 fig. 176:21, or ibid., 230:1, 2(G).

f. Wheelmade. Sand. Fine paste, buff core. Brown paint. *125*.

g. Wheelmade(?). Faience. Med-fine paste. Green-white. *119*.

h. Wheelmade. Lime. Med-fine paste, cream. *210*

i. Wheelmade(?). Lime + chaff. Med-fine paste, grey. *96*.

j. Handmade(?). Lime. Med. paste, orange-cream. Incised decoration. *98*.

k. Handmade. Grit. Coarse-med. paste. Grey inside wall, buff outside wall. Red paint. *155*.

l. Handmade. Lime + some grits. Coarse-med. paste, buff, cream exterior. Incised. *98*.

m. Wheelmade. Lime. med-fine paste, buff-cream, w. green walls due to high (second?) firing. Hind quarters of animal and 'metopes' in black paint. *33*.

7.0 *Other Finds*. A small number of objects other than pottery were encountered and deserve mention here.

7.1 Egyptian Hieroglyphic inscription on an alabaster sherd (fig. 7a, b). The fragment was seen at Tall Laylān (no. 44), and measured ca. 11 × 6 × 1 cm.[18] Mr. B. Garthoff of the Egyptological Seminary of the University of Amsterdam has kindly provided the following transcription and comment, working from a photograph.

> "Alabaster vessel fragment containing parts of three columns of Egyptian hieroglyphs, separated by two vertical incised lines, to be read from right to left, from top to bottom. The breaks and lacunae preclude a coherent interpretation.
>
> *col. 1*: t n wnt imjt = ". . ?. . ? baldness(?)"
>
> or: ṯ n wn ẖ'rt imjt = ". . ?. . ? the widow who is in(side)..."
>
> the latter reading is to be preferred, as the fem. determinative can probably be emended.
>
> *col. 2*: -Ḥr didi ʿ.wy m-ḥ't = "Horus who stretches both arms before...". probably the god Horus is meant; "who stretches both arms" could signify an offering. The Horus name of a king or a personal name is ruled out.
>
> On orthographical grounds the fragment cannot be dated before ca. 2000 BC, but greater precision is impossible".

7.2 A small (2.5 × 2.5 × ca. 1.5 cm.) baked clay tablet with cuneiform inscription was found by a local farmer at the foot of Qalʿat al Hādī (site no. 155) and was subsequently bought for the Syrian Antiquities Service by our representative Mr. S. Yunan (fig. 8a). Although the site in question lay outside the boundaries of the survey, publication here is warranted. Dr. J. D. Hawkins of London kindly provided the copy, transliteration and translation, based on seeing the tablet itself which was shown to him by Mr. Yunan early in 1978:

Old Babylonian record tablet

Transliteration	*Translation*
1. 58$\frac{1}{3}$ MA.NA KÙ.BABBAR	58$\frac{1}{3}$ minas of silver
2. up-pu-úš-ma	—it is computed
3. 3 li-mi 5 me GÍN KÙ.BABBAR	as 3500 shekels of silver*—
4. ša i-na ^{giš}PISAN qú-pi(?)	which from the box-container(?)
5. i-na ^{na4} KIŠIB e-wa-ri	under the seal of Ewari
6. ù ^{lú}eb-bu-tim^{meš}	and the trustees

[18] The object remained in the possession of the villager who brought it to our attention.

7. ^{lú}ḫa-ab-ba-ti-i$^{⌜\text{meš}?⌝}$	the robbers
8. ka-aš-⌜du?⌝	have acquired(?);
9. 1$\frac{1}{2}$ MA.NA 5 GÍN GUŠKIN	1$\frac{1}{2}$ minas and 5 shekels of gold
10. 58 GÍN u_4-nu-ut ZABAR	58 shekels of bronze equipment

The date formula on the edge of the tablet is unreadable (D.M.)

7.3 Tall Bayandūr (no. 6) produced a brown limestone statue, to parallels of which Dr. E. Porada and especially Dr. T.H. Carter drew the writer's attention [19]. It measures ca. 32 × 16 cm. (height × frontal width) and represents a squat anthropoid with an owlish face. Possibly to be dated after the middle of the second millennium BC. Fig. 7c.

7.4 A white chalcedony stamp seal was seen at Qunayṭra (no. 27), measuring ca. 3.5 × 2 cm. on the flat surface bearing the picture (fig. 8b) representing a standing figure under a canopy. Probably Sasanian. No parallels found.

7.5 Impression of a cylinder seal on a pottery sherd (fig. 9). The sherd is from a wheelmade vessel, lime-tempered; green-cream fine paste. The maximum height of the impression is 2.8 cm.; the length of one rolling is 3.7 cm., therefore the diameter of the seal must have measured ca. 1.18 cm. The figures are well-defined, due to deep incisions in the (possibly soft, like wood or shell?) seal material: 'Nordsyrischer Kerbschnittstil, cf. Kühne 1980[a]: 36-43. A standing unclothed human figure with 'hollow' head grasps a horned quadruped (antilope or gazelle) by the snout with the left hand; small recumbent animal in between, another above back of quadruped: probably geese. Fillers of triangular impressions of engraver on the seal. For the feathers of the birds, cf. Buchanan 1966 no. 764, from Brāk. Date ca. 2500 BC. The object was found at T. Muḥ. Kabīr (no. *231* b).

7.6 *Lithic Industry*. No certain aceramic settlements have been found during the survey (cf. 8.0); hence the samples of obsidian and chert illustrated here from ceramic sites, most of which had pottery from the historical periods: sites no. 7, 96, 106, 144 and 145[a]. Cf. fig. 28-30.

[19] Cf. T.H. Carter, Expedition 12 1970 22-40. The object has already been illustrated by M.N. van Loon, Persica X 1982 pl. VI D. It remained with the villager who showed it.

8.0 *Results*. Regional surface surveys are by their nature not thorough enough to cover every small piece of flint or pottery. On the other hand, it is felt that the present survey has not left many sites larger than ca. 50 × 50 × 1 m. unnoticed (and these probably mainly in the region north of the road Qamis͟hlī-Malkīya, where the terrain is more difficult to traverse and survey); concerning smaller sites three remarks must be made:

1) sites of pre-chalcolithic cultures tend to be small;
2) chipped stone industry products are hard to find in recently plowed land; and
3) the area under consideration has been plowed and cultivated for over 4000 years, increasing the possibility that low, small camp sites have been erased.

These reasons mainly explain the lack of pre-pottery sites in our catalogue.

8.1 In general, surface surveys give only *prima facie* evidence that certain ceramic (or other) cultures are lacking. Upon excavation, these may nevertheless prove to be present. The positive attestation of a ceramic (or other) culture, on the other hand, is a valuable result of any survey. These results may be viewed in a wider context; but in the present case two things must be remembered. First, that the surveyed area does not constitute an ecological unity and hence cannot be used, without additional information, to form balanced hypotheses concerning, e.g., settlement patterns and subsistence in antiquity, or to perform a meaningful nearest-neighbour analysis. Second, the uncertain dating of some sherds and the accidental overlooking of others are disturbing factors which make conclusions based on ceramic statistics extremely hazardous. One can think of any number of correlation analyses, such as site size with chronological period. But as sherds picked up non-systematically on a mound of a certain size do not imply that the pertaining culture is present over the whole site, such analyses would be premature in the present context. Hence, as relative sizes during one period or the lack of a culture period at a site cannot be ascertained, tendencies toward, e.g., urbanization cannot be illustrated by this material. The graph of fig. 10 is thus necessarily only a tentative representation of the development of settlement distribution.

8.2 With all these cautionary remarks in mind, the following observations may perhaps be permitted.

8.2.1 Although many sites lie along wadis, a respectable number do not; hence it must be inferred that also in antiquity wells were dug from the earliest periods onwards, as was certainly the case by Byzantine times [20].

[20] Gra-i Mirka (no. 126) produced a water well with a stone masonry lining from that period. Of the more recent ones, some reach a depth of 35 m. Cf. site no. 141.

8.2.2 No true Hassuna or Samarra wares have been encountered, which is remarkable in view of their relative frequency south-east of the Djabal Sindjār (cf. D. Kirkbride, Iraq 34 1972:3).

8.2.3 In a short note on the first two seasons of survey (Meijer 1978/9), we provisionally concluded that Halaf and Ubaid sites seemed to be restricted mainly to the Taurus foothills. Upon completion of the fieldwork, this proved to be untrue (cf. fig. 31); if any distinction can be made between the two areas mentioned in 1.1—the northern hills and the southern plain—it is that occupation in the north was generally less dense than in the south. This probably reflects a preference for the richer soils in the southern area.

8.2.4 Some 90% of the sites with Ubaid wares also have Halaf pottery, whereas the reverse is not true; this manifests a decrease in the number of settlements from Halaf to Ubaid.

8.2.5 The relative peak in sites with Uruk-, Gawra- or Amuq F - related wares (cf. fig. 10) forms an interesting background for the discussion about the spread of the 'Uruk and Gawra Cultures' to the north and west. The recent finds of 'Uruk' temples at Djebel 'Arūda (van Driel 1983) and Qannās (Finet 1979), both on the Euphrates, and in Tall Hammām on the Balīkh (van Loon and Meijer, in press) can be compared to the long-known buildings of Gawra XIII-VIII (Tobler 1950) dating to the Ubaid and Uruk periods. Whereas the architectural similarity between these sites seems to suggest a measure of cultural unity between ca. 3600 and 3000 BC., a slightly more complicated picture is presented by the pottery: the sites on the Euphrates produced a ceramic assemblage quite comparable to that of the type-site Uruk (Sürenhagen 1978), while the Amuq (OIP 61), Ḥammām (l.c.), Brāk (Fielden 1981: 160) and our survey sites seem to reflect a northern tradition (where, however, the 'classical' Uruk could be imported, cf. site no. 11, fig. 16h), which has ties with Gawra XI^{A}-VIII. It is hoped that an analysis of the pottery from Tall Laylān will shed light on this problematic situation, from which two provisional conclusions can be drawn: architecture and ceramic tradition do not have to run parallel as culture indicators, if this point needed stressing; and in the specific case of the Uruk/Gawra period, the local North Syrian ceramic tradition seems to remain virtually unaffected by an assemblage probably imported from the south-east and restricted to sites along the Euphrates, suggesting that the Euphrates was the main traffic lane for the Uruk culture. A balanced evaluation of the cultural influence spheres as indicated by pottery and architecture will also have to consider the sealings on tablets or bullae from Djebel 'Arūda (van Driel 1983), Ḥabūba Kabīra (Heinrich 1973), Ḥammām (van Loon and Meijer, in press), Gawra (Tobler 1950: pl. LXXXIX^{a}), Brāk (? Oates 1982: pl. XV^{c}), and Nineveh (Collon and Reade 1983), as well as the apparent absence of 'beveled rim bowls' at Ḥammām and Gawra. The cautious remarks by van Driel (1983:58) regarding the sealings and their comparability are noted, but to judge from the drawings there seems to be a remarkable similarity between the Iranian (cf., e.g., Amiet 1972, Weiss and Young 1975), Mesopotamian and Syrian motifs and their execution, suggesting intensive commercial contacts during a restricted period between these areas. Whether such contacts were concomitant with deepening cultural ties such as religion (as suggested by temple plans), or whether they were no more than relatively superficial intrusive incidents in a solid 'local culture'[21], remains one of the most pressing problems to be solved by controlled excavations.

8.2.6 Some 62% of the sites identified as having EB III pottery also contain the so-called 'Metallische Ware' (Kühne 1976). Nos. 210 (Farfara), 72 (Gēr Suwār) and 82 (Gēr Shirān) produced much of this (but see 6.3.2).

8.2.7 No direct archaeological links with either Assur or Kültepe can be demonstrated. Tell Laylān (site no. 44, Weiss 1981/2) has both unpainted Middle Bronze pottery and Khabur ware, along with many other wares. If one should want to study the chronological or functional relation between unpainted Middle Bronze pottery and Khabur ware, site no. 125 would offer a good opportunity.

8.2.8 The great majority of sites measure less than 2 hectares. This number, together with a height of at least 15 m., has been chosen arbitrarily as the minimum size for the following list of sites.

site no.	ha.	site no.	ha.
4	6.6	119[a]	4.8
5	15.0	122	5.4
6	4.1	124	6.2
12	5.0	125	6.4
14	6.0	134	4.0
15	6.0	139	3.5
21	8.3	140	6.4
23	5.6	146	9.1
24	9.6	148	4.6
41	5.5	157	43.0
44	90.0	163	6.2
49	4.0	168	4.3
51	9.0	169	6.4
53	6.2	171[a]	11.6
63	3.0	175[a]	2.0
72	5.1	205	98.0
82	3.8	210	106.3
94	6.0	231[b]	12.0

[21] In that case the similarity of public buildings (so far without cone-mosaic decoration, excepting Brāk) must be ascribed to other factors.

96	6.8	251	46.0
98	10.9	277	2.0
106	2.0	282	2.8
116	3.4	283	2.3
118	11.6	289	20.0[22]

It can be seen that ca. 13% of the sites are larger than this arbitrary minimum. Only four of these (nos. 63, 94, 171[a] and 175[a]) produced *no* MB pottery. The sites over 10 ha. in area over ca. 15 m. in height are nos. 5, 44, 98, 118, 157, 171[a], 205, 210, 231[b], 251 and 289; they all lie in the southwesterly part of the surveyed area, undoubtedly because the geomorphology is responsible for the relative abundance of water there. Some clustering of smaller sites around the larger ones may be observed, but as has been noted (cf. 8.1), we hesitate to draw conclusions from this. A notable fact is that the larger sites tend to lie along the still existing major tracks (e.g., nos. 5, 6, 12, 15, 140, 23) or along the main wadis (e.g., along the D̲jag̲hd̲jag̲h and the D̲jarrāḥ).

8.2.9 Although the ware-frequency chart (fig. 10) shows a decline in sites towards the Iron Age, historical evidence for the Late Bronze Age[23] furnishes no ready explanation or even illustration of this phenomenon, e.g. in the way of population decrease or tendencies toward centralization[24]. Especially in the Neo-Assyrian period, the area is often mentioned; for this and the preceding Late Bronze Age, controlled excavations such as now under way at Tall S̲h̲ayk̲h̲ Ḥamed are urgently needed. The results of our survey concerning these periods are undoubtedly skewed by imperfect knowledge of their ceramic traditions. No 'Nuzi Ware' was found.

8.2.10 If only by virtue of its size, Tall S̲h̲arīsi (no. 205) is worth a thorough investigation.

[22] Sites 154-156 were left out of the list, as they lay outside the area surveyed or because the numbers wer discarded. For 166 see site cat.

[23] Most recently, see Kessler 1980; the archaeological evidence seems to find support in remarks by Dobel et. al. (see note 7, p. 264) and Kühne (AfO 25 1974-77 254).

[24] The recent discovery of a fortress like Dūr Katlimmu (Kühne 1981/2) may suggest, however, that a central authority attempted to provide temporary safety for regional setllers in times of trouble, possibly with a view towards binding them politically.

9.0 *Conclusion.*

The main purpose of the survey was to obtain a corpus of data regarding the area under discussion, that might help toward solving archaeological and historical problems by pinpointing the most promising sites for future excavation. Even without excavation, it is clear from fig. 10 that the Middle Bronze Age (ca. 2000-1600 BC), with four times the number of Early Bronze IV or Late Bronze Age sites, witnessed a peak of occupation that can only be explained by external factors. There is a strong suspicion that this peak is due to the impact of Old Assyrian trade on the regions through which is passed, and the Khabūr basin is shown to hold considerable promise for increasing our knowledge of that phenomenon.

List of Sites per Pottery Category.

PRE HALAF etc.
(code 1)
42, 63, 68, 96, 106, 170[a], 197, 242[b], 282

HALAF etc.
(code 2)
7, 15, 16, 23, 25, 58, 61, 63, 71, 85, 106, 140, 145[a], 163, 188. 190, 192, 197, 207, 224[a], 231[b], 235, 237, 239, 242[b], 245, 261, 273[a], 273[b], 273[c], 284, 289

UBAID etc.
(code 3)
15, 16, 23, 25, 58, 61, 63, 71, 92, 96, 140, 142, 145[a], 146, 163, 183, 188, 192, 207, 224[a], 231[b], 235, 242[b], 261, 273[a]

URUK etc.
(code 4)
11, 25, 53, 61, 71, 80, 82, 88[a], 92, 94, 96, 106, 110, 126, 142, 146, 163, 190, 197, 210, 231[b], 242[b], 245, 268, 273[b], 282, 289

EB I
(code 5)
23, 44, 53, 71, 82, 96, 106, 163, 171[a], 210, 231[b], 282

5a (Nin. V)
7, 27, 33, 44, 53, 96, 106, 171[a], 230, 231[b], 277, 282, 289

EB II
(code 6)
23, 44, 53, 82, 92, 96, 106, 163, 175[a], 210, 239, 243[a], 282

EB III
(code 7)
1, 5, 6, 12, 23, 44, 53, 56[b], 57, 58, 71, 72, 73, 82, 83, 85, 92, 94, 96, 98, 106, 109, 122, 126, 134, 156, 157, 163, 169, 171[a], 175[a], 195, 202, 205, 210, 212, 231[b], 234[a], 239, 243[a], 246, 251, 261, 277, 282, 283, 286, 288[a], 288[b], 289

7a (Metallische Ware)
5, 6, 44, 45[a], 53, 56[b], 57, 71, 72, 82, 85, 91[b], 94, 96, 98, 106, 118, 126, 134, 137, 156, 157, 169, 171[a], 175[a], 206, 210, 231[b], 246, 251, 282, 283, 286, 289

EB IV
(code 8)
5, 14, 15, 18, 24, 38, 44, 45[a], 46, 53, 56[a], 56[b], 57, 69, 72, 73, 83, 96, 98, 101, 106, 108, 122, 125, 128, 129, 134, 139, 160, 166, 168, 176, 194, 195, 202, 204, 205, 210, 212, 231[b], 231[c], 242[b], 243[b], 251, 273[a], 277, 281, 282, 285[a], 289

MBA
(code 9)
2, 4, 5, 6, 8, 12, 14, 15, 16, 18, 22, 23, 24, 26, 32, 33, 34, 37, 38, 41, 43, 44, 45[a], 46, 47, 49, 52, 53, 56[b], 59, 69, 72, 73, 80, 82, 86, 87, 89, 91[b], 92, 93, 96, 98, 101, 102, 103, 104, 105, 106, 107[a], 108, 109, 116, 117, 118, 119[a], 121, 122, 123, 124, 125[!], 129, 130, 131, 134, 139, 140, 141, 143, 144, 146, 148, 149, 151, 157, 160, 163, 164[a], 166, 168, 169, 171[a], 178, 179, 182, 184, 192, 193, 195, 196[a], 196[b], 199, 201, 202, 203[a], 203[c], 204, 205, 206, 207, 208[b], 209, 210, 211, 212, 217, 218[b], 219, 220[a], 220[b], 220[c], 221[a], 221[b], 224[b], 226, 228, 229, 230, 231[a], 231[b], 233, 235, 236, 237, 238, 239, 241, 242[a], 243[b], 245, 246, 250, 251, 253, 255, 257, 258, 259, 261, 262, 263, 265, 266, 267, 270, 271, 273[b], 273[c], 274, 275, 276, 277, 279, 282, 283, 284, 285[a], 285[b], 286, 289

9a (Habur)
1, 4, 6, 7, 8, 12, 14, 18, 19, 21, 23, 24[a], 32, 33, 37, 38, 40, 41, 43, 44, 46, 49, 51, 52, 53, 56[b], 58, 67, 71, 72, 79, 80, 82, 86, 87, 89, 92, 93, 96, 98, 99, 102, 106, 107[a], 109, 110, 116, 118, 119[a], 119[b], 121, 124, 125[!], 126, 128, 129, 134, 139, 140, 144, 146, 148, 151, 157, 160, 163, 156, 168, 179, 192, 196[a], 201, 205, 207, 210, 217, 218[a], 229, 231[b], 237, 246, 251, 258, 259, 267, 277, 283, 284, 285[a], 289

LBA
(code 10)
8, 14, 38, 44, 47, 49, 51, 90, 95, 98, 102, 104, 109, 110, 118, 121, 134, 139, 146, 150, 153, 166, 168, 169, 186[b], 205, 210, 216, 219,

220[c], 222, 227, 231[a], 234[b], 251, 262, 268, 289

IRON A.
(code 11)
14, 41, 68, 72, 75, 90, 99, 101, 107[b], 115[a], 121, 134, 187[b], 193, 195, 210, 215[a], 231[a], 236, 263, 266

HELL.-ROM.-PARTHIAN
(code 12)
5, 14, 51, 72, 75, 98, 110, 161, 164[b], 173[a], 174[b], 183, 216, 231[b], 245, 276, 283, 289

BYZ.
(code 13)
1, 10, 12, 13, 17, 20, 27, 28, 30, 39, 48, 50, 53, 54, 63, 64, 65, 66, 75, 76, 84, 100, 102, 113, 114, 115[a], 141, 144, 145[b], 147, 152, 160, 161, 163, 164[b], 165, 167, 174[b], 175[c], 177, 204, 205, 207, 217, 221[a], 230, 236, 244, 245, 263, 264, 286, 290

'ISLAMIC'
(code 14)
10, 15, 17, 20, 21, 22, 23, 24[a], 27, 28, 29, 30, 31, 34, 35, 39, 41, 45[a], 50, 51, 52, 54, 55, 59, 64, 65, 66, 75, 77, 81, 83, 84, 88[b], 91[a], 97, 99, 100, 110, 111, 116, 119[a], 127, 132, 135, 138, 144, 145[b], 146, 147, 151, 152, 161, 162, 164[b], 167, 172[a], 172[b], 173[b], 177, 180, 184, 186[b], 187[a], 189, 198, 200, 202, 204, 207, 208[a], 214[a], 221[b], 223, 232, 240, 244, 248, 252, 254, 256, 260, 264, 266, 269[a], 270, 272, 275, 276, 278, 279, 280, 287, 289

Site Index

Gra-i Rēsh 1
Gunduk 73
Gunduk Sayyid 120
Ḥabāra Ṣaghīra 235
Ḥabāra Kabīra 240
Ḥaddādīya 225
Ḥadjar 15
Ḥadjdjī Baḍr 171
Ḥadjdjī Kabīr 203[a]
Ḥadjdjīya Kabīra 200
Ḥadjdjīya Ṣaghīra 201
Ḥalimūk 18
Ḥallāq 33
Ḥamāra 109
Ḥāmis 258
Ḥamū 48
Ḥamūkār 156
Ḥarb 185
Ḥaṣuratlī 138
Ḥashnīya 22
Ḥumaydī 251
Ḥumaydī 278
'Ibrahīm al Maḥmūd 241
'Īd 166
Karakilise 28
Kharāb Badjar 152
Kharāb al Baghāl 75
Kharāb al Darīsiāt 221
Kharnūb 3
Khatūn 7
Khazimūk 13
Khazna 66
Khazna Kabīra 63
Khazna Ṣaghīra 64
Kharaydjka I 69
Kharaydjka II 70
Khirbat Dība 54
Khirbat Djamū 237
Khirbat Djiḥāsh 115
Khirbat Ḥmara 110
Khirbat Khalīl 62
Khirbat Khazna 190
Khirbat Lazāqa 135
Khirbat Ma'rūf 92
Khirbat Mardjānī 114
Khirbat Mas'ūda 197
Khirbat Qarāṣa 113
Khirbat al Qaṭa 31
Khirbat Sabība 100
Khirbat al-Sāda 260
Khirbat al-Simm 132
Khirbat Ṣūfīya 117
Khirbat Tafl 266
Khuwaytla 216
Khuwaytla 253
Kirk Khazna 36
Kīta 232
Kubayba 93
Laylān 44
Lazāqa 137
Luks 26
Ma'bada 38
Maqrināt 133
Ma'rūf 91
Mastī 261
Mas'ūda 198
Ma'shūq 16
Mathlawtha 'Arīḍa 101
Ma'az 286
Mazra'at Tuwayyim 242[b]
Maḥarqān 10
Mahum 23
Maṣīla 272
Muzayrīb 59
Miḍrī 29
Mīr 'Azaziāt 42
Mashrīfa Saghīra 254
Mashrīfa Kabīra 255
Mukīnīya 204
Muḥammad Kabīr 231[b]
Muḥammad Ṣaghīr 231[a]
Muḥammad Diyāb 118
Nabū'a 121
Na'idj 102
Na'matlī 2
Niṣr 51
Naṣrān 87
Nidjmūk 275
Qabr Aḥmad al Sahīm 50
Qaḥṭanīya 11
Qal'at al Hādī 155
Qarāṣa 98
Qarghū 32
Qarḥū 145
Qaṣīr 47
Qaṣmīya 149
Qaṣr 105
Qaṣr al Dīb 41

Fukhkhariya: C. W. McEwan e.a., Sounding at Tall Fakharīyah. Chicago 1958.
Halawa: W. Orthmann, Halawa 1977-1979. Bonn 1981.
Hama: E. Fugmann, Hama. L'Architecture des Périodes Pré-Hellénistiques. København 1958.
Mardikh: P. Matthiae, Ebla, Un impero ritrovato. Torino 1977.
OIP: R. and L. Braidwood, Excavations in the Plain of Antioch I. Chicago 1960.

Bell, G.	1911	Amurath to Amurath. London.
Buchanan, B.	1966	Catalogue of Ancient Near Eastern Seals in the Ashmolean Museum, vol. I. Oxford.
Collon, D. and J. Reace	1983	Archaic Nineveh. *Baghdader Mitteilungen 14:33-41.*
Çulpan, C.	1975	Türk Taş Köprüleri. Ankara.
Davidson, T. and McKerrell, A.	1976	Pottery Analysis and Halaf Period Trade in the Khabur Headwaters Region. *Iraq XXXVIII:45-56.*
Delougaz, D.	1952	Pottery from the Diyala Region. Chicago.
Dillemann, L.	1962	Haute Mésopotamie orientale et pays adjacents. Paris.
Dussaud, R.	1927	Topographie Historique de la Syrie antique et Médiévale. Paris.
Fielden, K.	1981	A Late Uruk Pottery Group from Tell Brak, 1978. *Iraq 43:157-166.*
Finet, A.	1979	Bilan provisoire des fouilles belges du Tell Kannas. *Annul of the American Schools of Oriental Research 44:79-95.*
Hallo, W.	1978	Simurrum and the Hurrian Frontier. *Revue Hittite et Asianique XXXVI:71-83.*
Hamlin, C.	1971	The Habur Ware Ceramic Assemblage of Northern Mesopotamia: an Analysis of its Distribution. (Diss.). Ann Arbor.
Heinrich, E. (e.a.)	1973	Vierter vorläufiger Bericht über die von der Deutschen Orient-Gesellschaft (...) unternommenen archäologischen Untersuchungen (...). *Mitteilungen der Deutschen Orient-Gesellschaft 105.*
Hrouda, B.	1957	Die bemalte Keramik des zweiten Jahrtausends in Nordmesopotamien und Nordsyrien. Berlin.
Hrouda, B.	1958	Waššukanni, Urkiš, Šubat-Enlil. *Mitteilungen der Deutschen Orient-Gesellschaft 90:22-35.*
Ilter, F.	1974	Güney-doğu anadolu erken devir türk köprülerinin yapisal ve süsleyici ögeler yönünden değerlendirilmesi. *Anadolu XVIII:31-45.* (English summary pp. 46-49).
Kessler, K.	1980	Untersuchungen zur historischen Topographie Nordmesopotamiens. Wiesbaden.
Kühne, H.	1976	Die Keramik von Tell Chuēra. Berlin.
Kühne, H.	1980a	Das Rollsiegel in Syrien. Tübingen.

Kühne, H. 1980b Zur Rekonstruktion der Feldzüge Adad-Nīrārī II, Tukulti-Ninurta II Aššurnasirpal II im Hābūr-gebiet. *Baghdader Mitteilungen 11:44-70.*

Kühne, H. 1981/2 Tell Šēḫ Ḥamad/Dūr-Katlimmu. *Archiv für Orientforschung XXVIII:233-235.*

Layard, A.H. 1853 Discoveries in the Ruins of Niniveh and Babylon. London.

Lebeau, M. 1983 La céramique de l'Age du Fer II-III à Tell Abu Danné. Paris.

Lines, J. 1954 Late Assyrian Pottery from Nimrud. *Iraq 16:164-167.*

Mallowan, M. 1936 Excavations at Chagar Bazar, and an Archaeological Survey of the Habur Region of North Syria. *Iraq III:1-86.*

Mallowan, M. 1937 idem, second Campaign. *Iraq IV:91-177.*

Mallowan, M. 1947 Excavations at Brak and Chagar Bazar, Syria. *Iraq IX:1-259.*

Matthers, J. (ed.) 1981 The River Qoueiq, Northern Syria, and its Catchment. Oxford.

Meijer, D.J.W. 1978/9 Archäologische Geländebegehung östlich des Ǧaġǧaġ. *Archiv für Orientforschung XXVI:172-174.*

Moortgat, A. 1959 Archäologische Forschungen der Max Freiherr von Oppenheim-Stiftung im nördlichen Mesopotamien 1956. Köln.

Oates, D. 1982 Excavations at Tell Brak, 1978-81. *Iraq XLIV*^{2}*:187-204* (cf. 205-219).

Oates, J. 1959 Late Assyrian Pottery from Fort Shalmaneser. *Iraq 21:130-146.*

Oppenheim, M. von 1899 Vom Mittelmeer zum persischen Golf durch den Hauran, die Syrische Wüste und Mesopotamien. Berlin.

Pecorella, P. and M. Salvini 1981/2 Tall Barri/Kaḫat. *Archiv für Orientforschung XXVIII:208-210.*

Pecorella, P. and M. Salvini 1982 Tell Barri/Kahat 1. Relazione Preliminare sulle campagne 1980 e 1981 a Tell Barri/Kahat, nel bacino del Habur. Roma

Perthuis, Comte de 1896 Le désert de Syrie, L'Euphrate et la Mésopotamie. Paris.

Poidebard, A. 1934 La Trace de Rome dans le désert de Syrie. Paris.

Ponikarov, V.P. 1966 The Geological Map of Syria. Damascus.

Sachau, E. 1883 Reise in Syrien und Mesopotamien. Leipzig.

Sarre, F. and E. Herzfeld 1910 Archäologische Reise im Euphrat und Tigris Gebiet. Berlin.

Sürenhagen, D. 1978 Keramikproduktion in Habūba Kabīrā Süd. Berlin.

(de) Thevenot 1682 Gedenkwaardige en zeer nauwkeurige reizen van den heere de Thevenot, uit het Frans vertaald door G. van Broekhuizen. Amsterdam.

Tobler, A. 1950 Excavations at Tepe Gawra, vol. 2. Philadelphia.

van Driel, G. and C. van Driel-Murray 1983 Jebel Aruda, The 1982 Season of Excavation, interim report. *Akkadica 33:1-26.*

van Driel, G.	1983	Seals and Sealings from Jebel Aruda 1974-1978. *Akkadica 33:34-62.*
van Liere, W. and J. Lauffray	1954/5	Nouvelle Prospection Archéologique dans la Haute Jezireh Syrienne. *Annales Archéologiques Syriennes 4/5:129-148.*
van Liere, W.	1963	Capitals and Citadels of Bronze-Iron Age Syria in their Relationship to Land and Water. *Annales Archéologiques Arabes Syriennes 13:109-122.*
van Loon, M. and D. Meijer	in press	Hammam et-Turkman on the Balikh: First results of the University of Amsterdam's 1982 Excavation. *Annales Archéologiques Arabes Syriennes.*
Weiss, H.	1981/2	Tall Lelān. *Archiv für Orientforschung XXVII:226-229.*
Weiss, H. and T.C. Young	1975	The Merchants of Susa. *Iran XIII:1-17.*
Wirth, E.	1971	Eine geographische Landeskunde. Darmstadt.

Key to Figures

1. Map of surveyed area.
2. a. site no. 41, Qaṣr al Dīb, facing NNW.
   b. site no. 98, T. Qarāṣa, f. ENE.
   c. site no. 124, T. Abū Ḥadjar, f. E.
   d. site no. 146, T. ʿAlū, f. ESE.
3. a. site no. 205, T. Sharīsi from afar, facing N.
   b. view from summit of Sharīsi, f. WSW.
4. Site no. 45 b, Djazīrat Ibn ʿUmar; consecutive views of the reliefs on the octagonal downstream side of the first pylon on the Syrian side of the river, going from SW through SE to NE.
5. Continuation of fig. 4.
6. a. Outline of site no. 205, T. Sharīsi.
   b. Outline of site no. 210, T. Farfara.
   c. Outline of site no. 251, T. Ḥumaydi.
7. a. Photograph of inscription on Egyptian alabaster fragment (cf. p. 43) found at Tall Laylān (site no. 44).
   b. transcription of a.
   c. Statuette from Tall Bayandūr (site no. 6); cf. p. 44.
8. a. Photographs and handcopy (by J. D. Hawkins) of obverse (upper) and reverse (lower) of tablet from Qalʿat al Hādī (site no. 155); cf. p. 43f.
   b. White chalcedony stamp seal from Qunayṭra (site no. 27); cf. p. 44.
9. Photograph and drawing (the latter by Mr. Jan de Wit) of cylinder seal impression on pottery sherd from T. Muḥ. Kabīr (site no. 231 b); cf. p. 44.
10. Graph showing frequency of sites per pottery category, as coded on p. 32.
11. Chronological table; cf. p. 32.

12-27. See pp. 34-43.

28. Lithic artifacts from site no. 96, T. Abū Khazaf. *a*. chert blade with traces of use ans sheen on cutting edge; bitumen traces on both front and back. *b*. chert blade with traces of use and sheen. *c*. chert, traces of use. *d*. obsidian, traces of use. *e*. obsidian, traces of use. *f*. obsidian, traces of use. *g*. obsidian, traces of use.
29. a. Obsidian blade with traces of use (site no. 106). *b*. obsidian blade with traces of use (106). *c*. brown grey chert blade with traces of use and sheen (106). *d*. chert blade with traces of use (site no. 7). *e*. obsidian blade fragment (site no. 145). *f-i* obsidian blade fragments from site no. 144.
30. From site no. 144. *a-c* flint blade fragments. *d*. obsidian blade.
31. Distribution map of Halaf pottery.
32. Distribution map of Uruk pottery.
33. Distribution map of EB III pottery.
34. Distribution map of MB pottery.

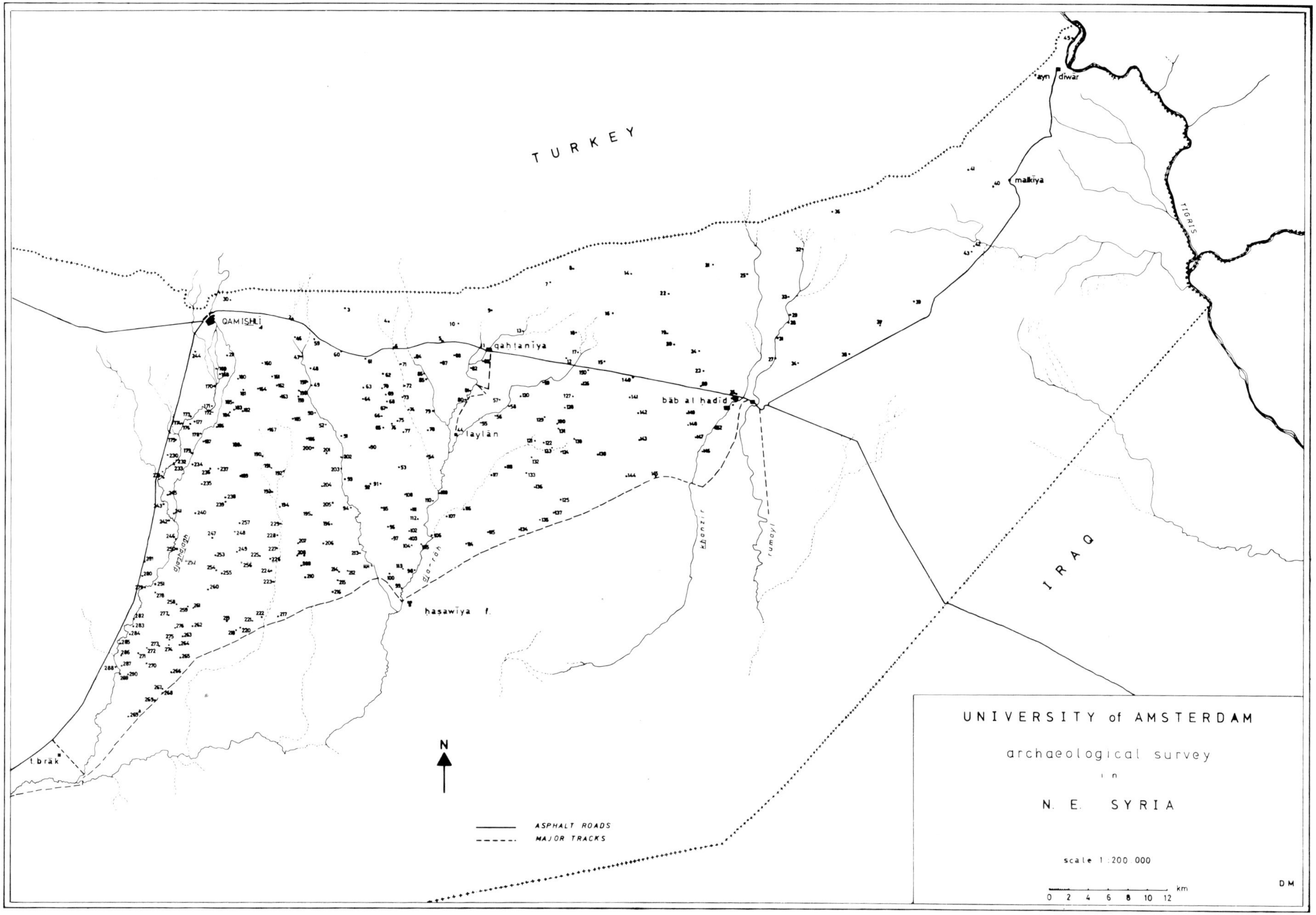
UNIVERSITY of AMSTERDAM
archaeological survey
in
N. E. SYRIA
scale 1:200 000
0 2 4 6 8 10 12 km
DM
ASPHALT ROADS
MAJOR TRACKS
N
TURKEY
IRAQ
TIGRIS
QAMISHLI
qahtaniya
laylan
bab al hadid
hasawiya
malkiya
ayn diwar
t.brak
khanzir
rumayl
djaghdjagh
dja-rah

FIGURE 1

a

b

c

d

FIGURE 2

a

b

FIGURE 3

FIGURE 4

FIGURE 5

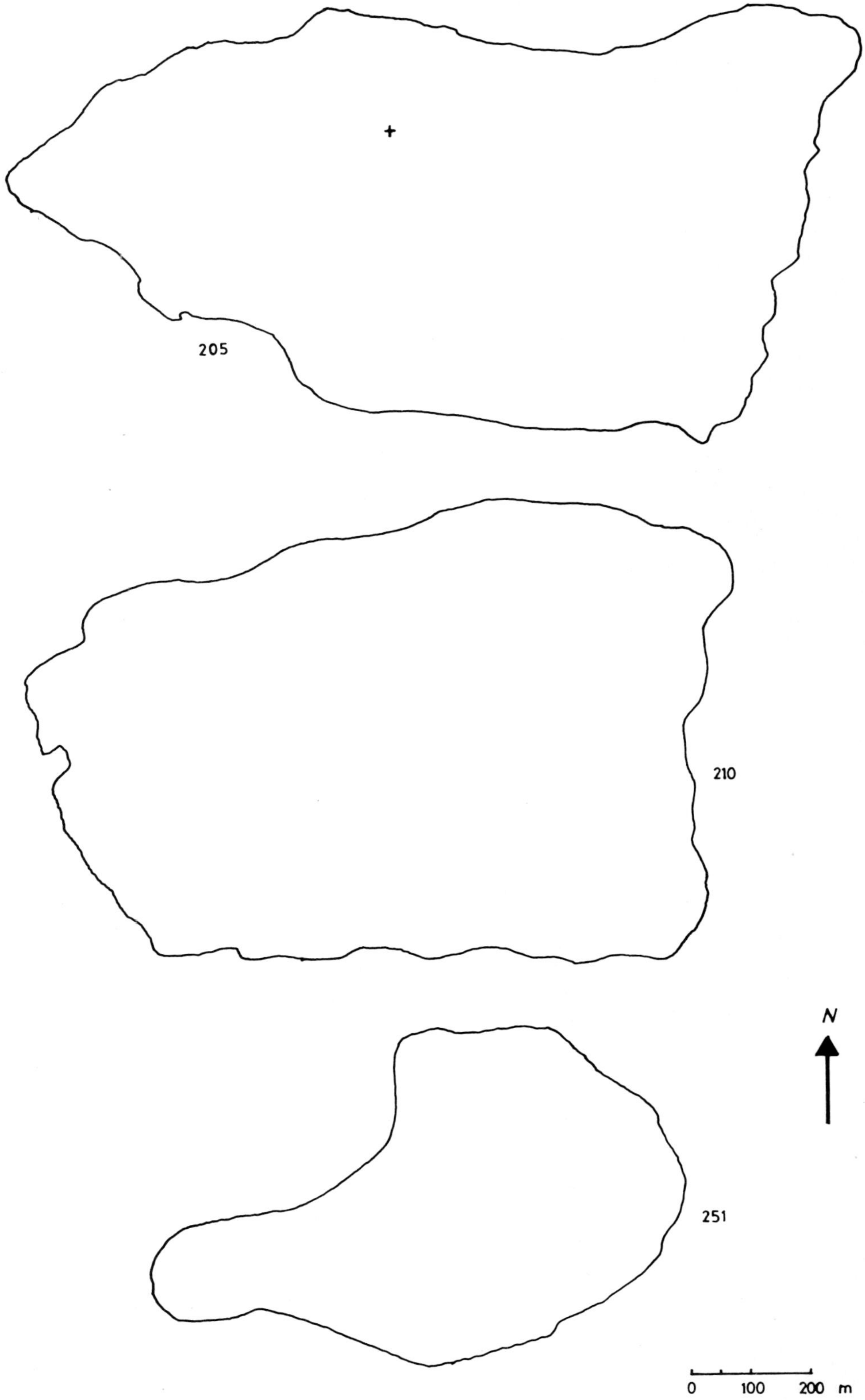

FIGURE 6

a

b

c

FIGURE 7

a

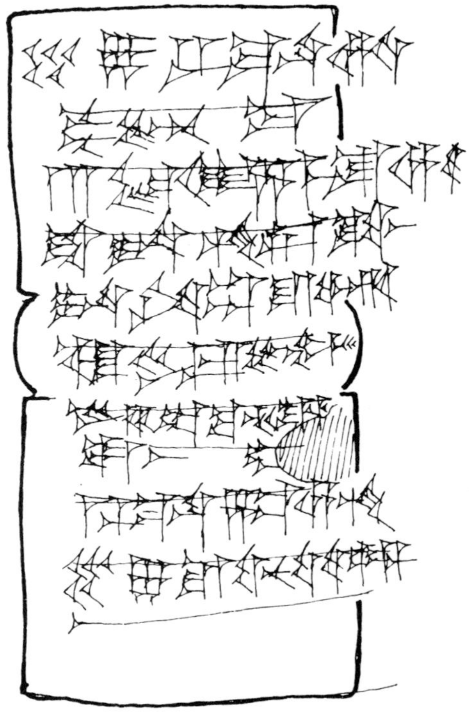

b

FIGURE 8

FIGURE 9

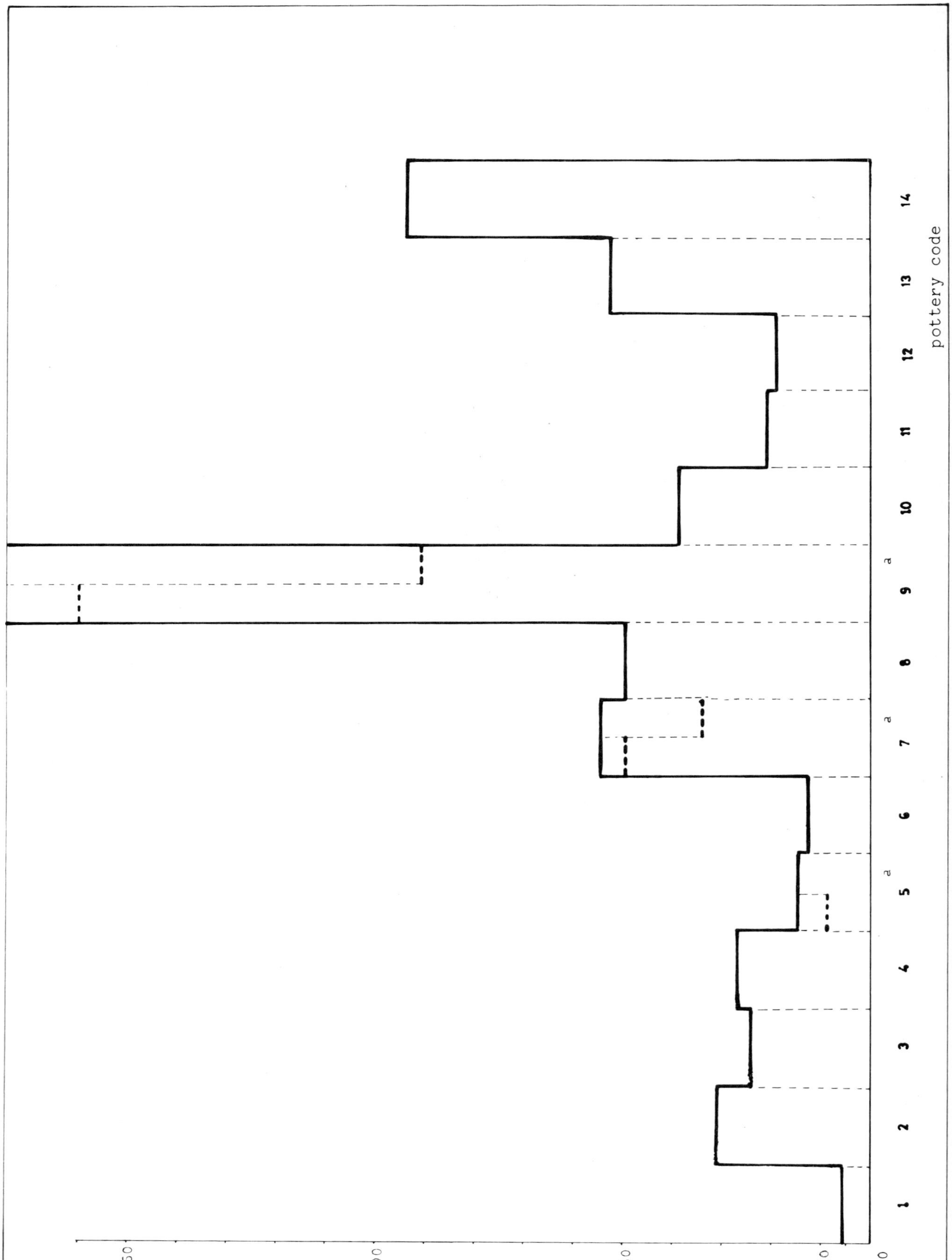
number of sites
pottery code
0
10
50
100
150
1
2
3
4
5
a
6
7
a
8
9
a
10
11
12
13
14

FIGURE 10

DATE BC	AMUQ	MARDIKH	HAMA	GAWRA	VARIA	PERIOD
5000	B					
4500	C					HALAF
4000	D		L			UBAID
3500	E					URUK
3400						
3300				XI		LATE URUK
3200	F			X		
3100		I a ?	K	IX		
3000		I b				
2900		?				EB I
2800	G			VIII		EB II
2700					Halawa Tall B	
2600		II a				
2500	H			VII		EB III
2400						
2300						
2200	I	II b 1	J	VI		
2100	J	II b 2				EB IV
2000						
1900		III a		V		MB I
1800	K		H		Halawa Q 2	
1700	L	III b		IV		MB II
1600						
1500				III		
1400	M		G	– ?		LB
1300						
1200						
1100	N					IRON I
1000			F			
900						IRON II
800			E			
700	O					
600						
500						IRON III

FIGURE 11

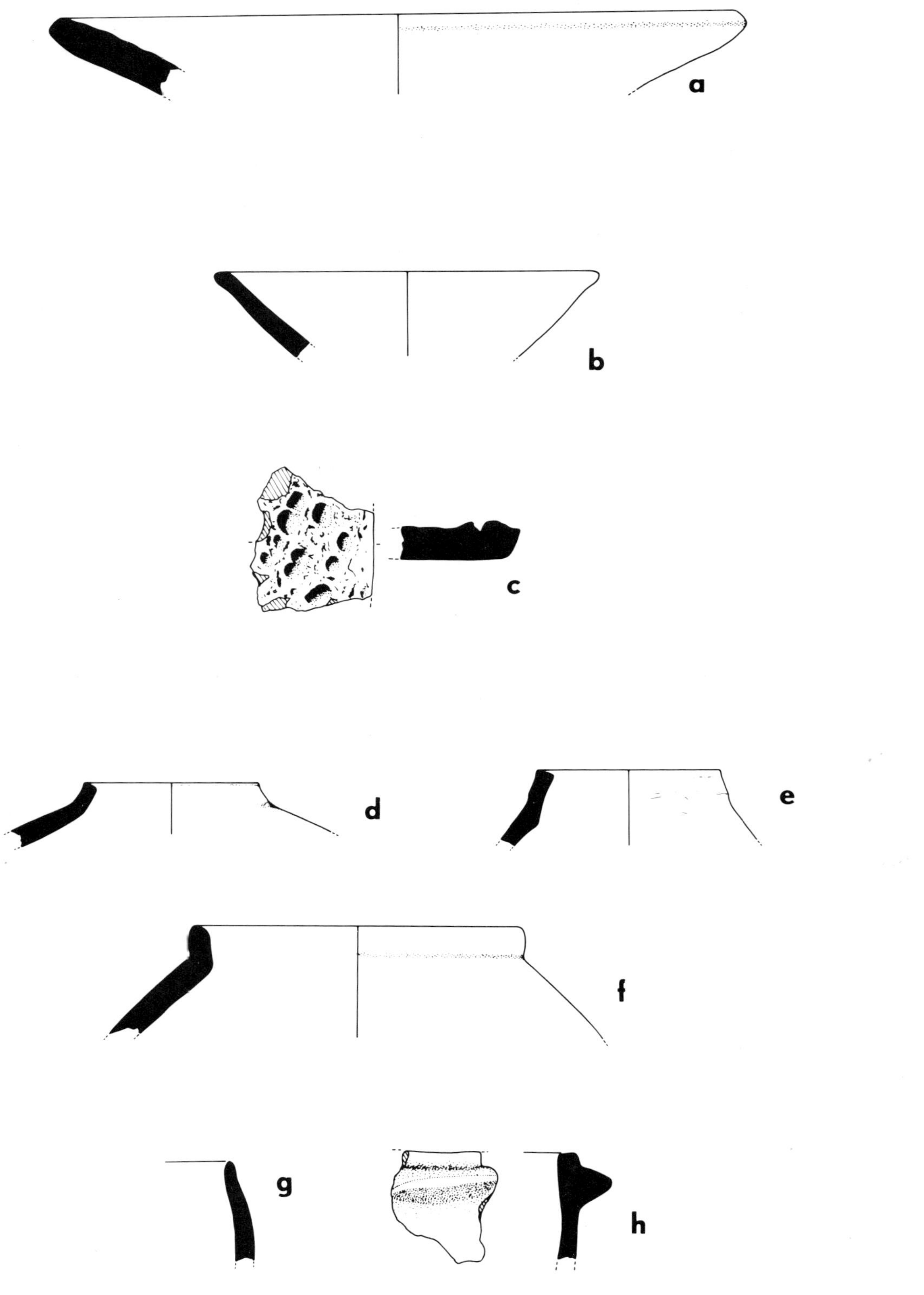

FIGURE 12

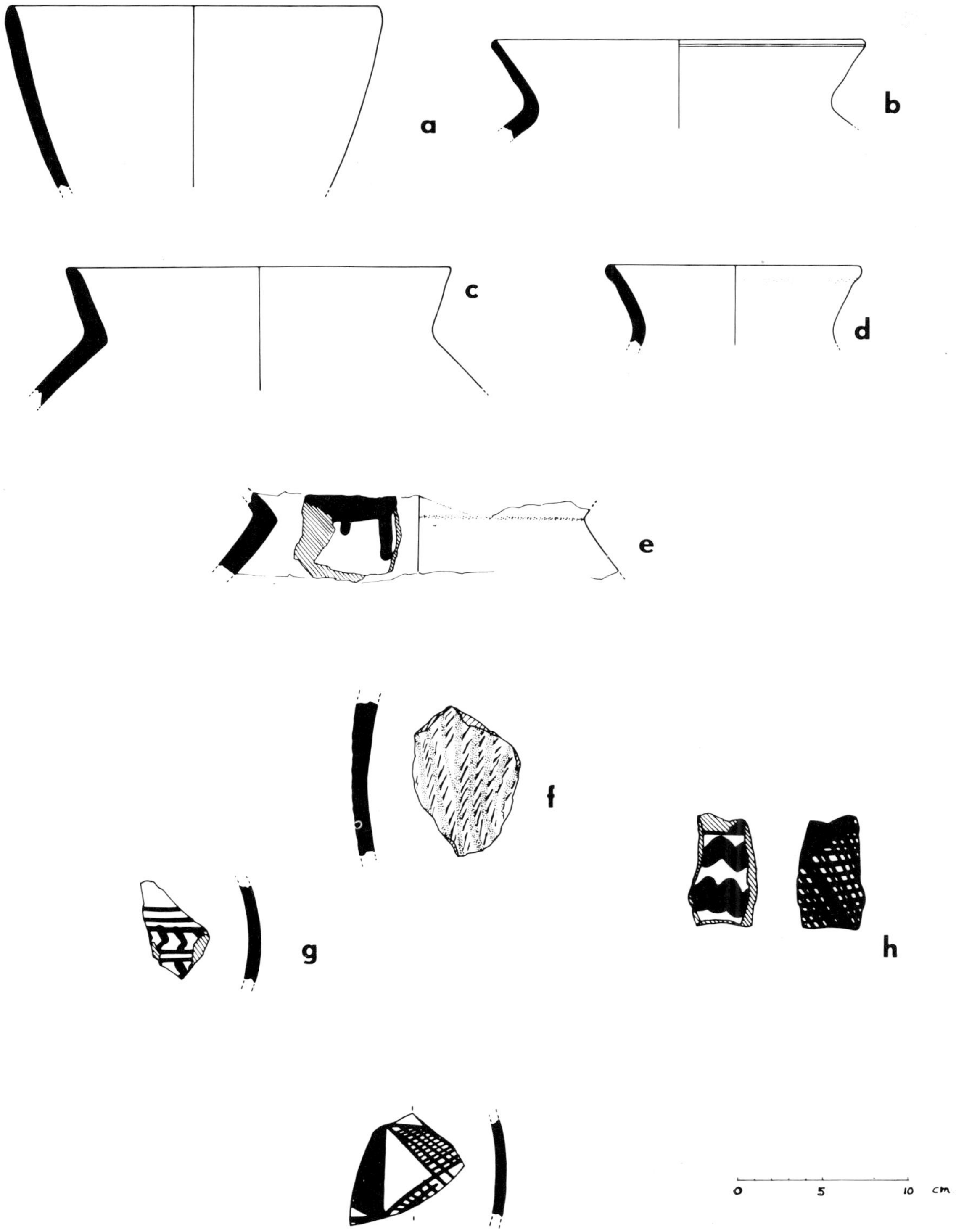

FIGURE 13

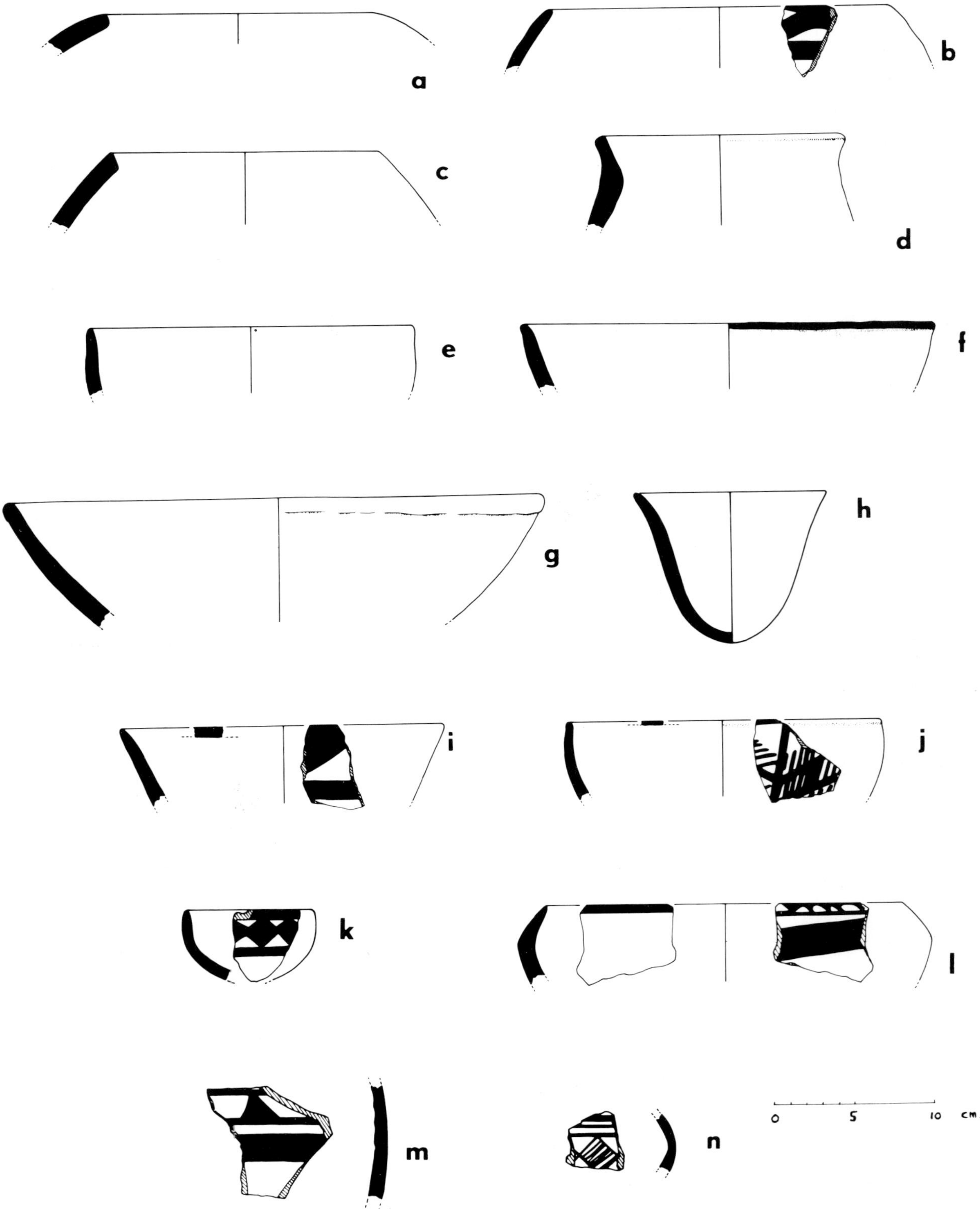

FIGURE 14

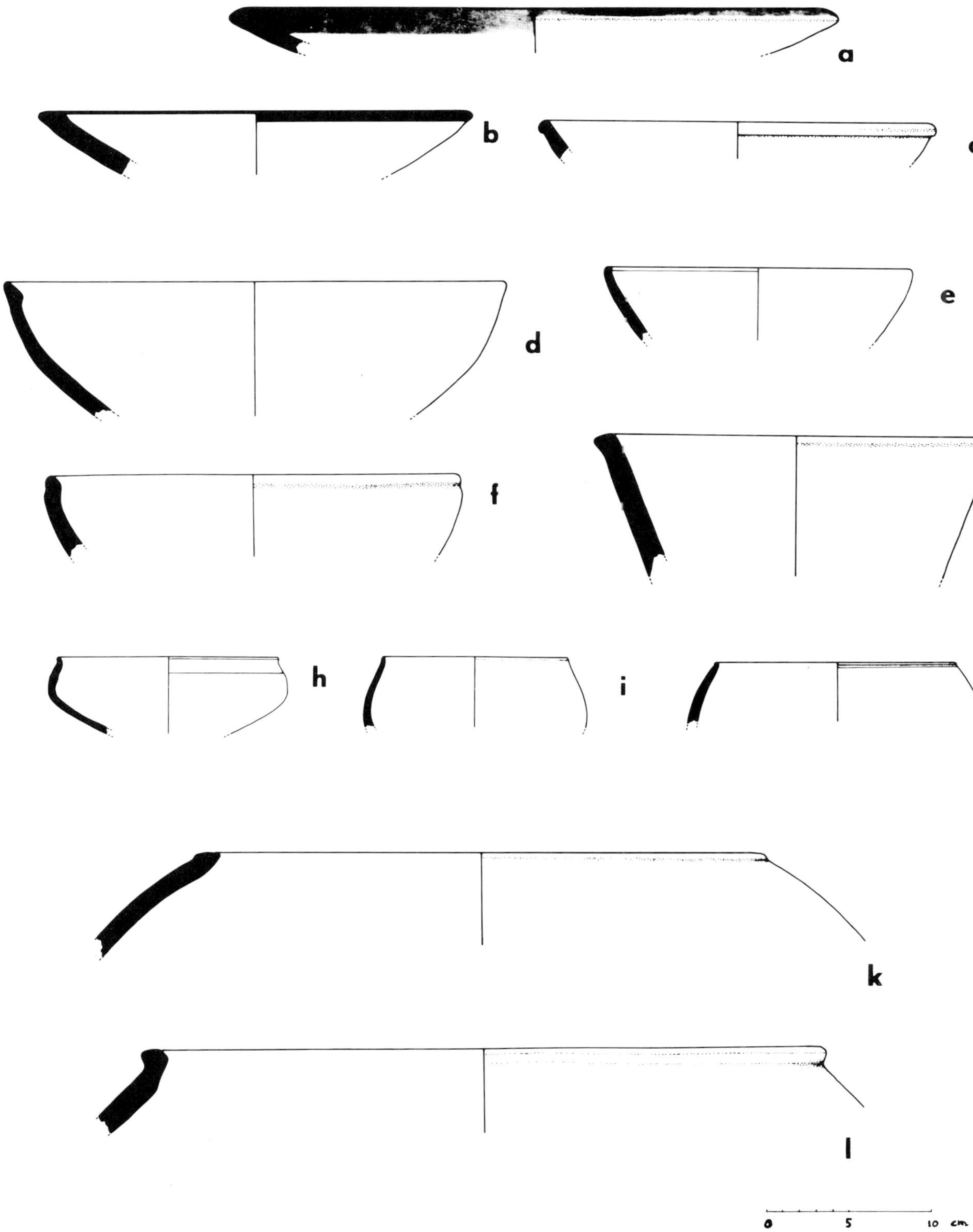

FIGURE 15

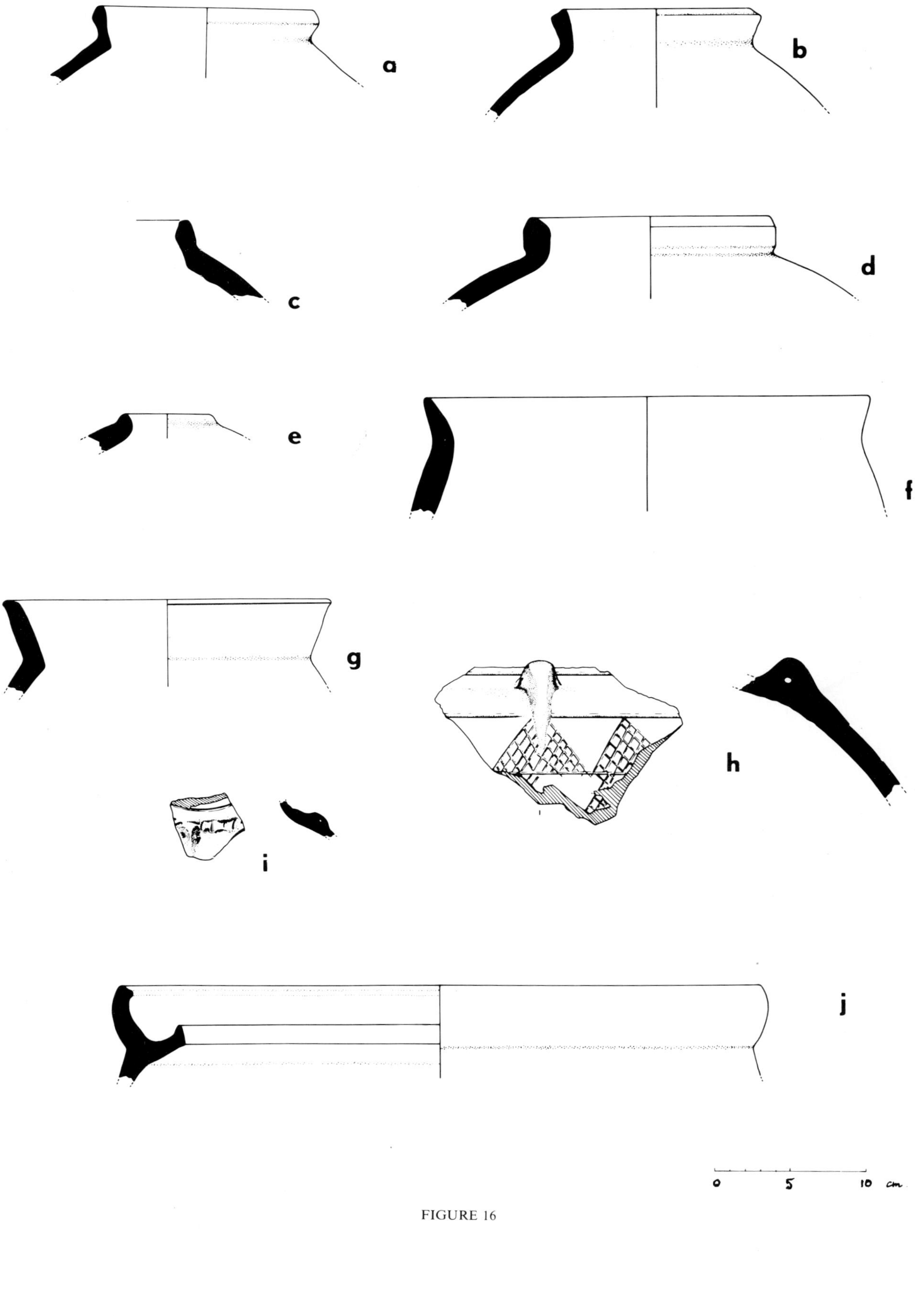

FIGURE 16

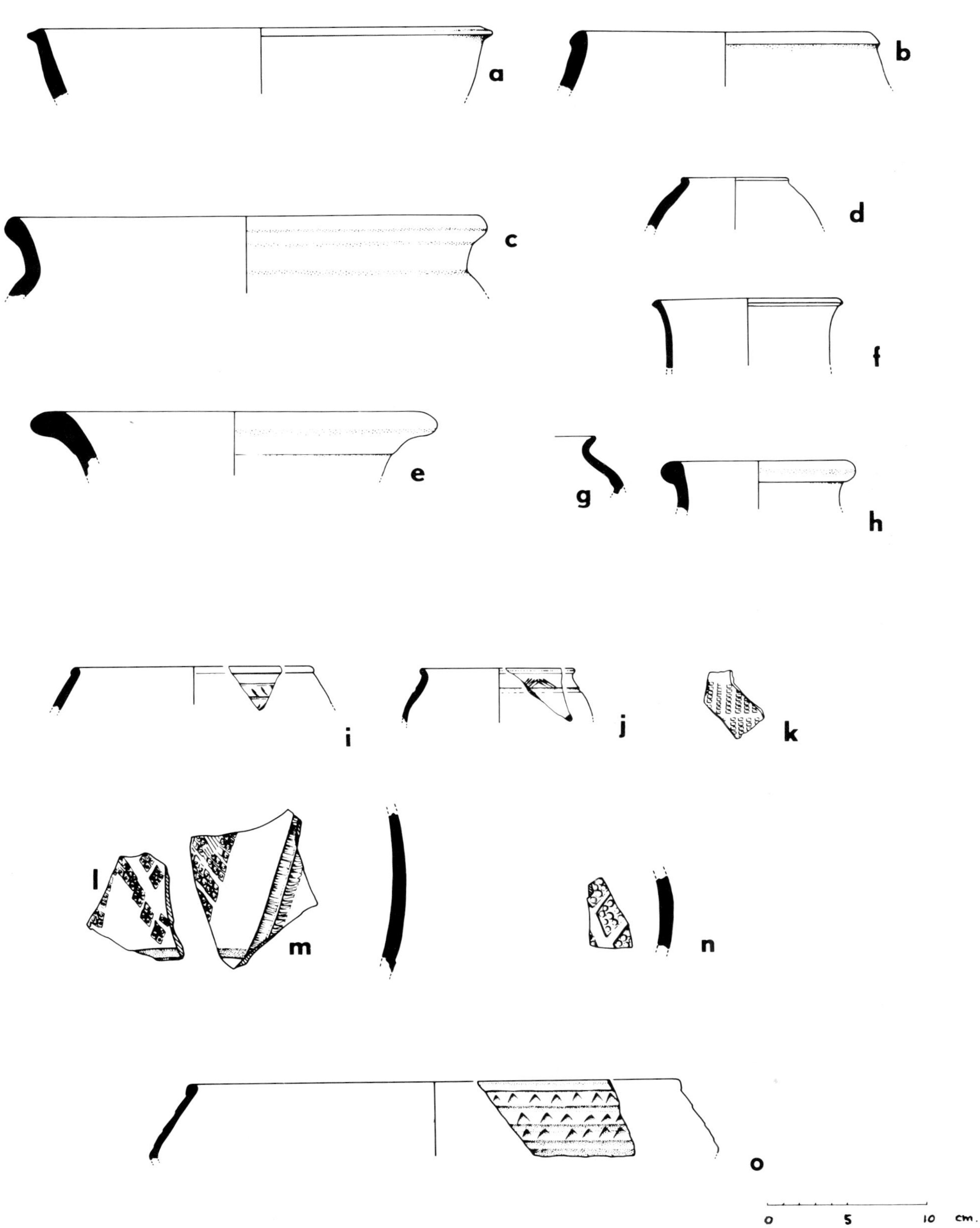

FIGURE 17

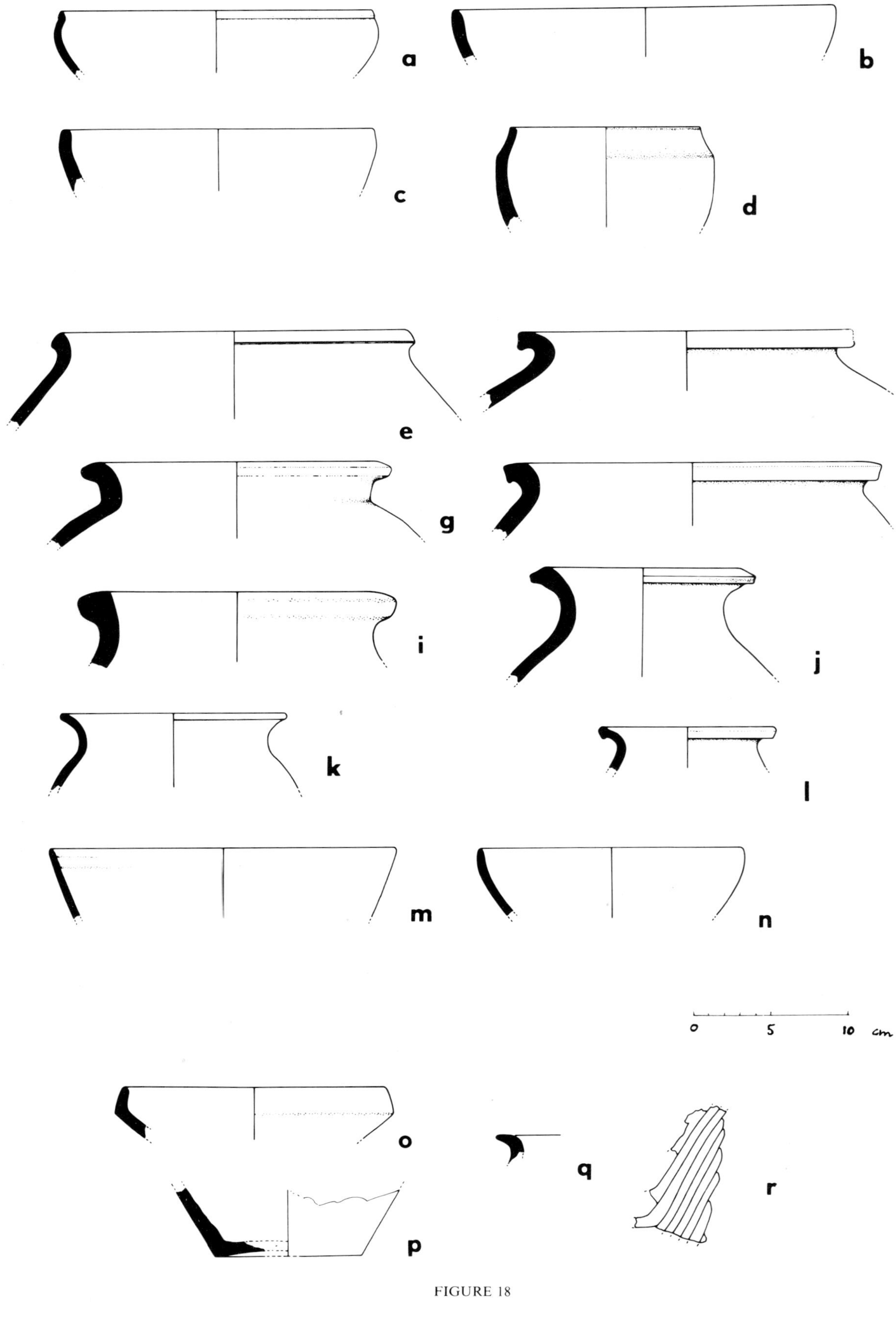

FIGURE 18

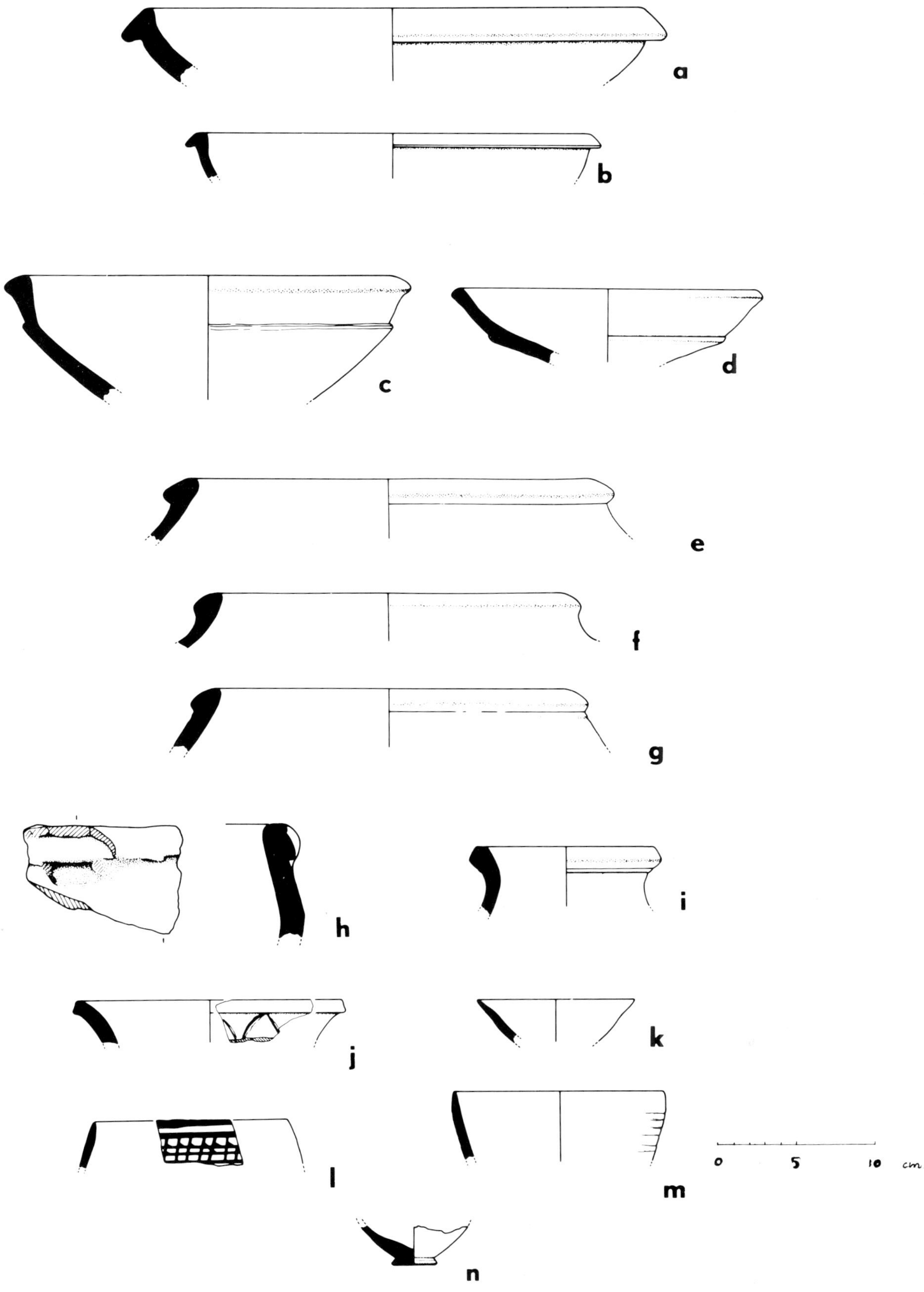

FIGURE 19

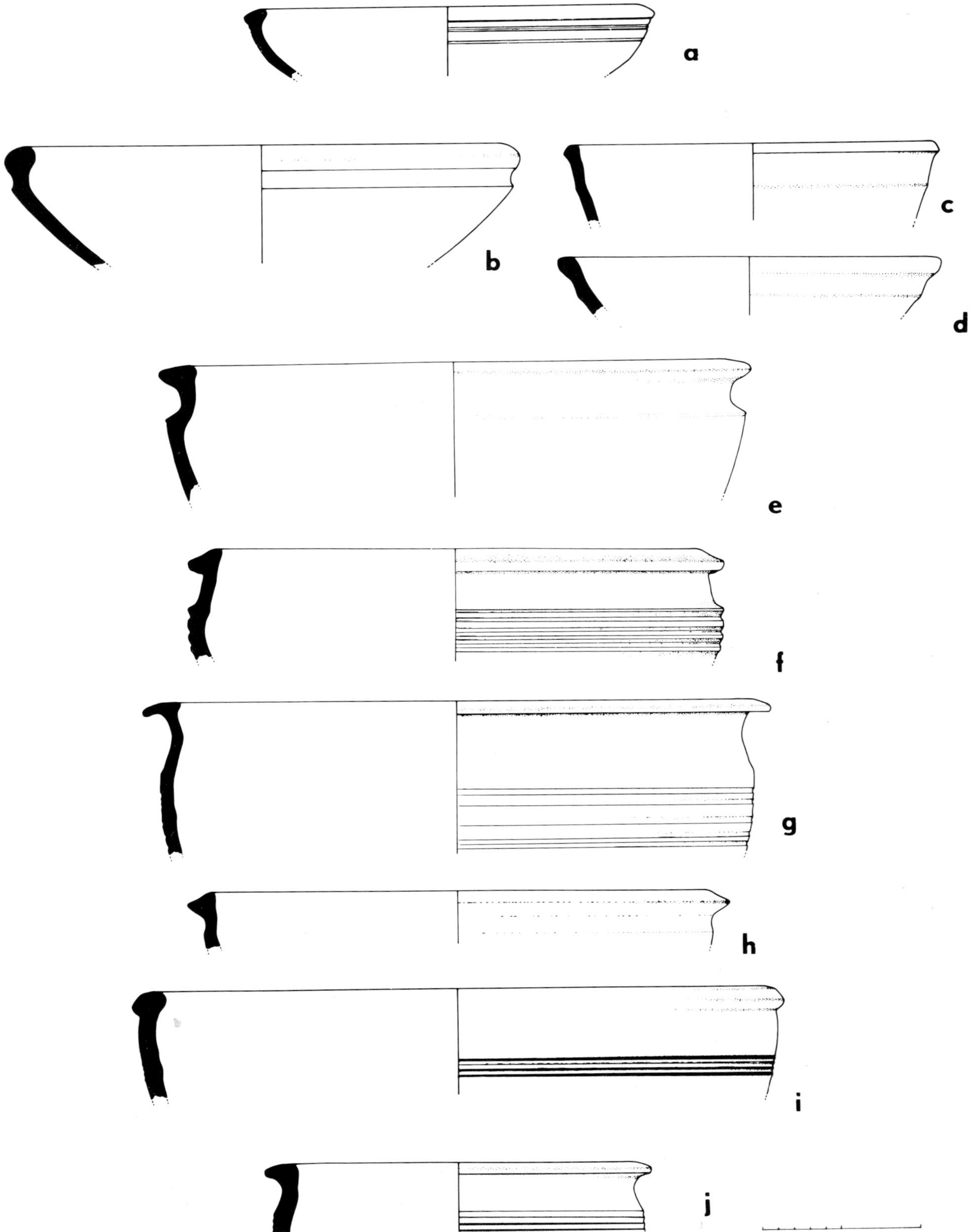

FIGURE 20

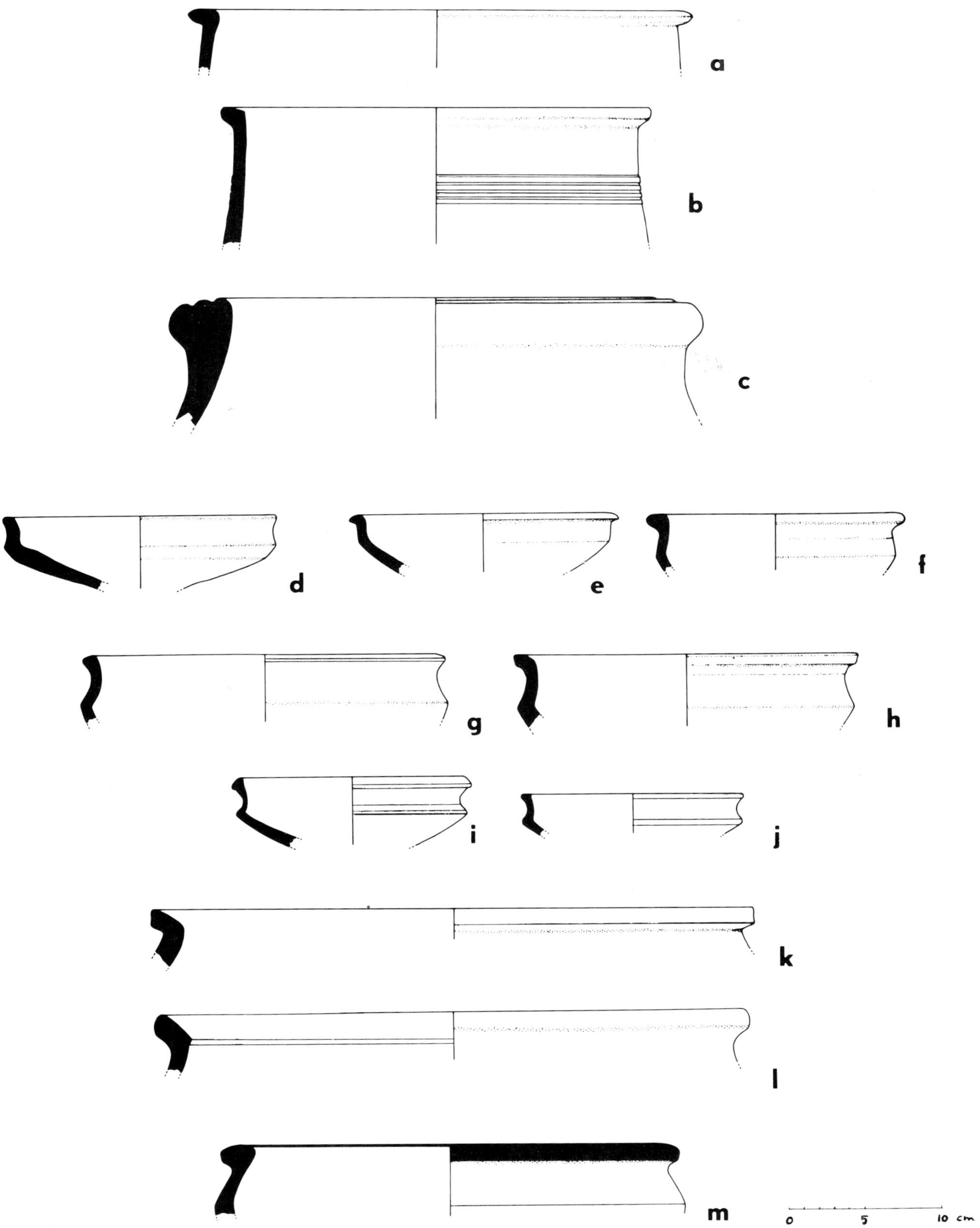

FIGURE 21

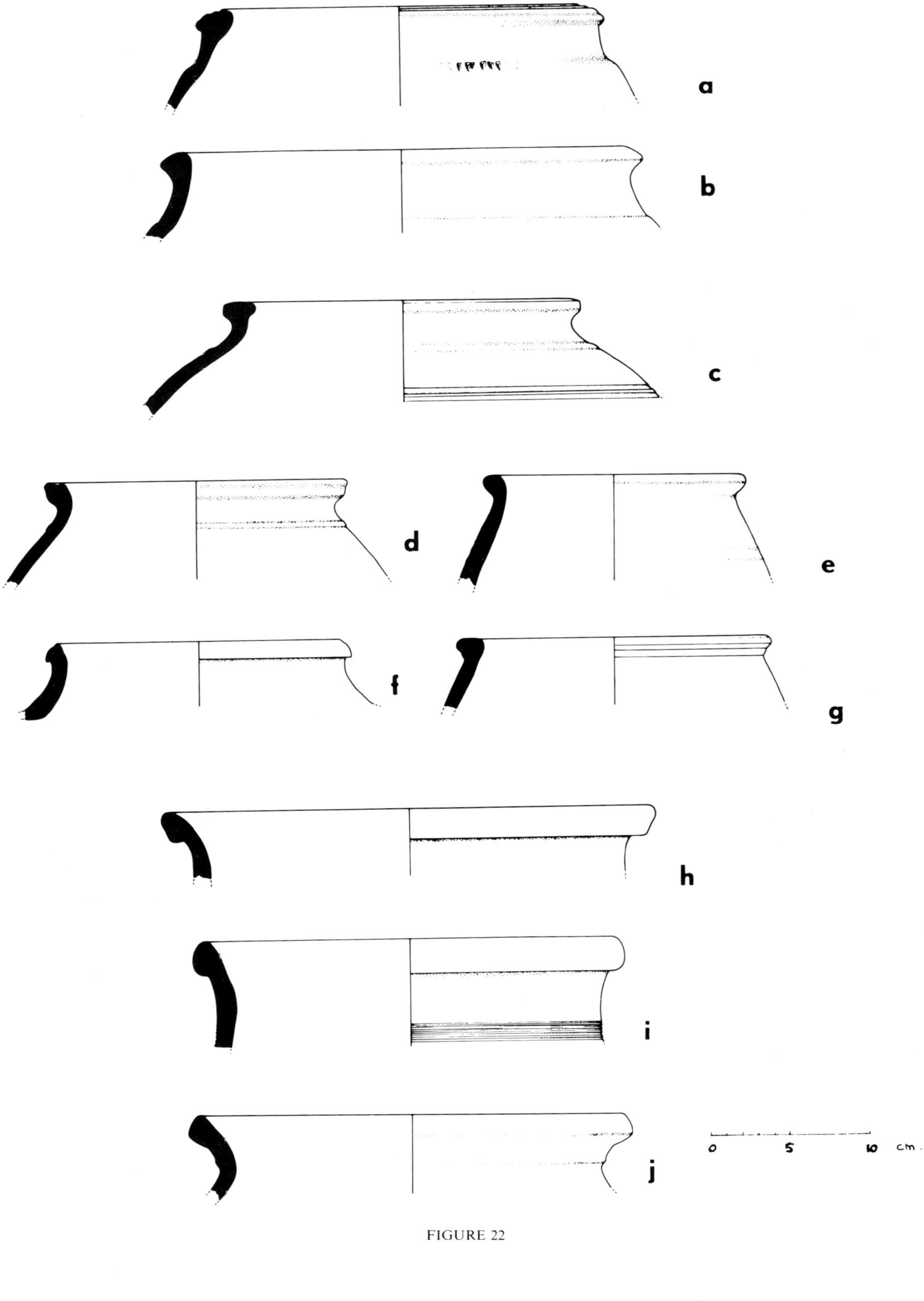

FIGURE 22

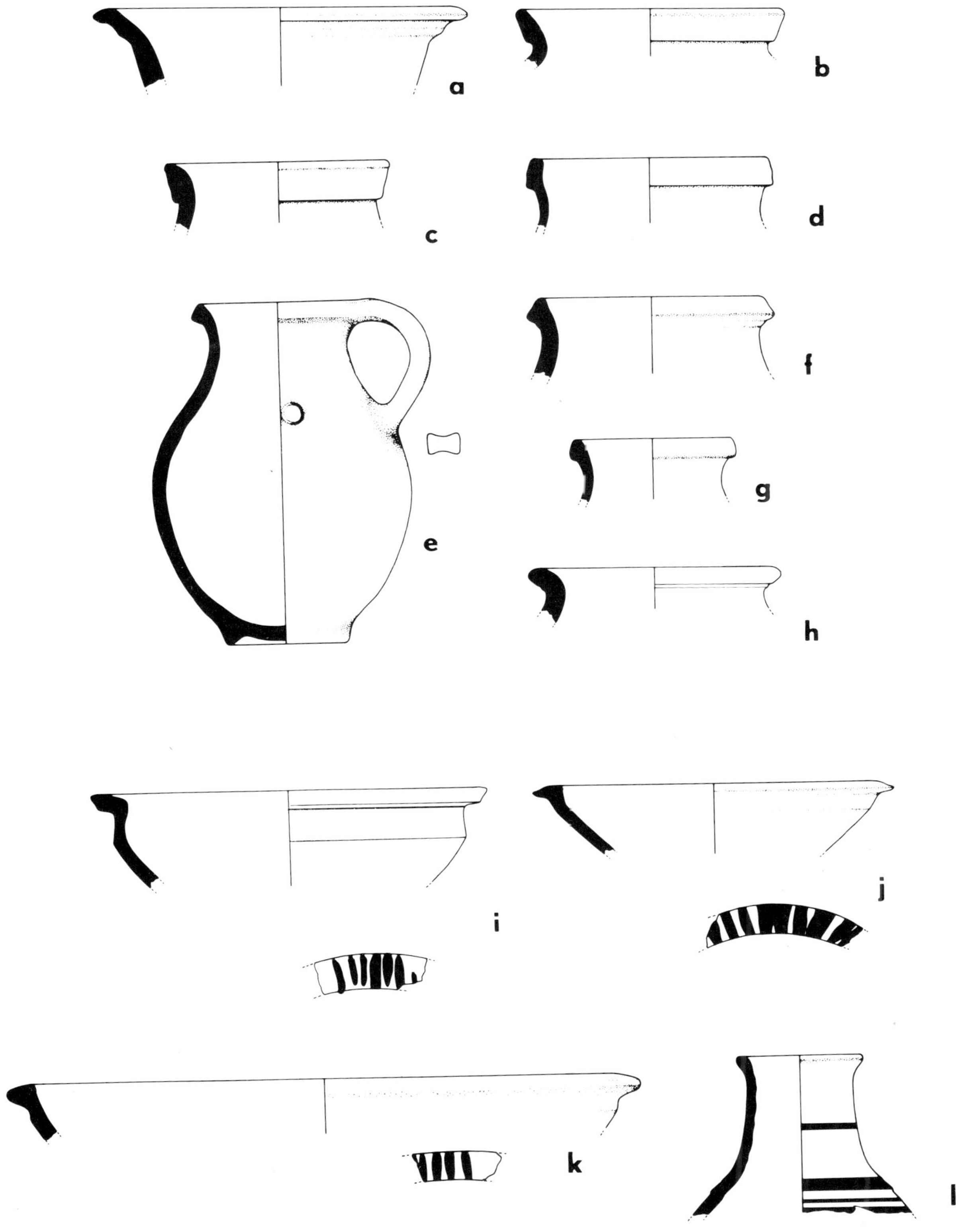

FIGURE 23

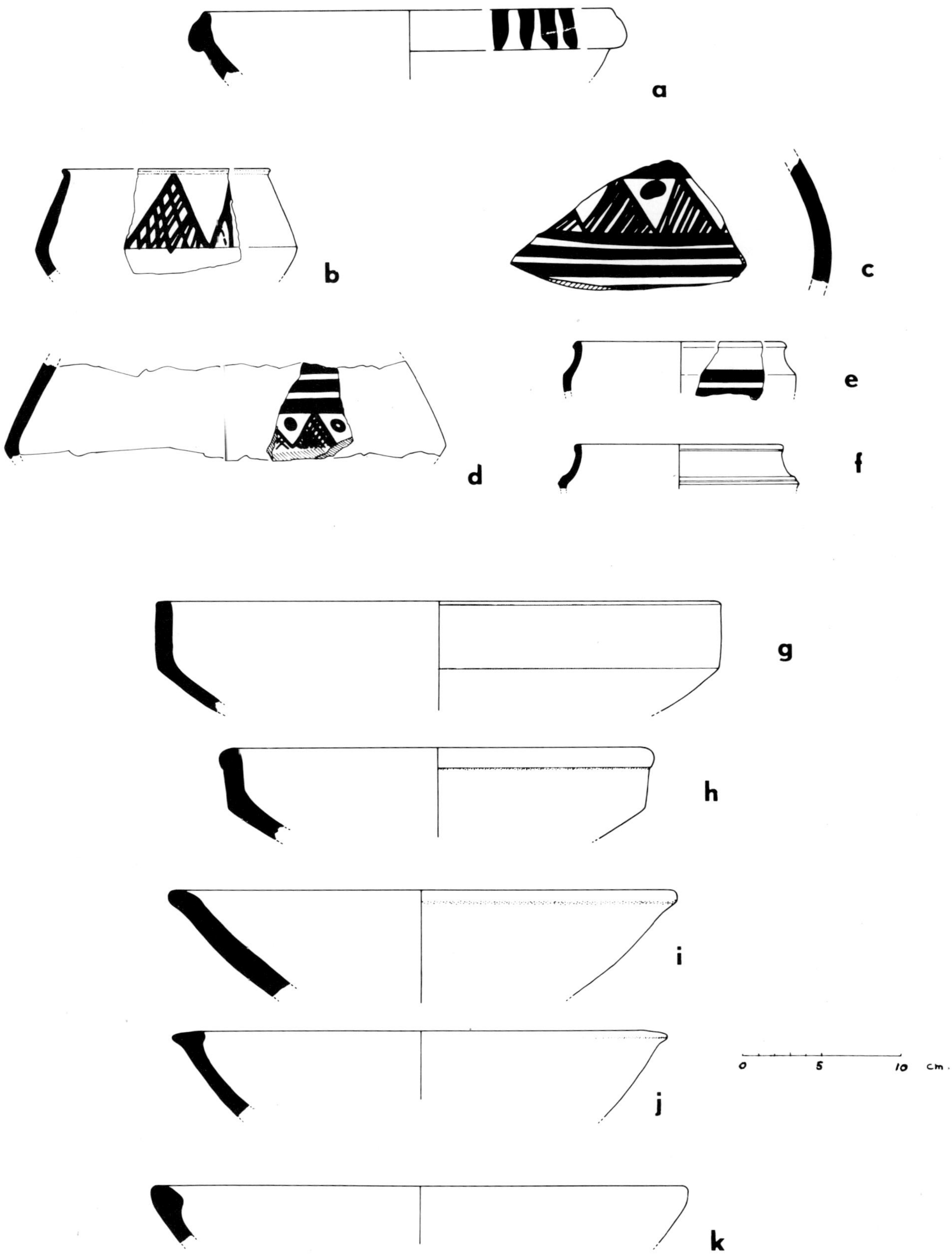

FIGURE 24

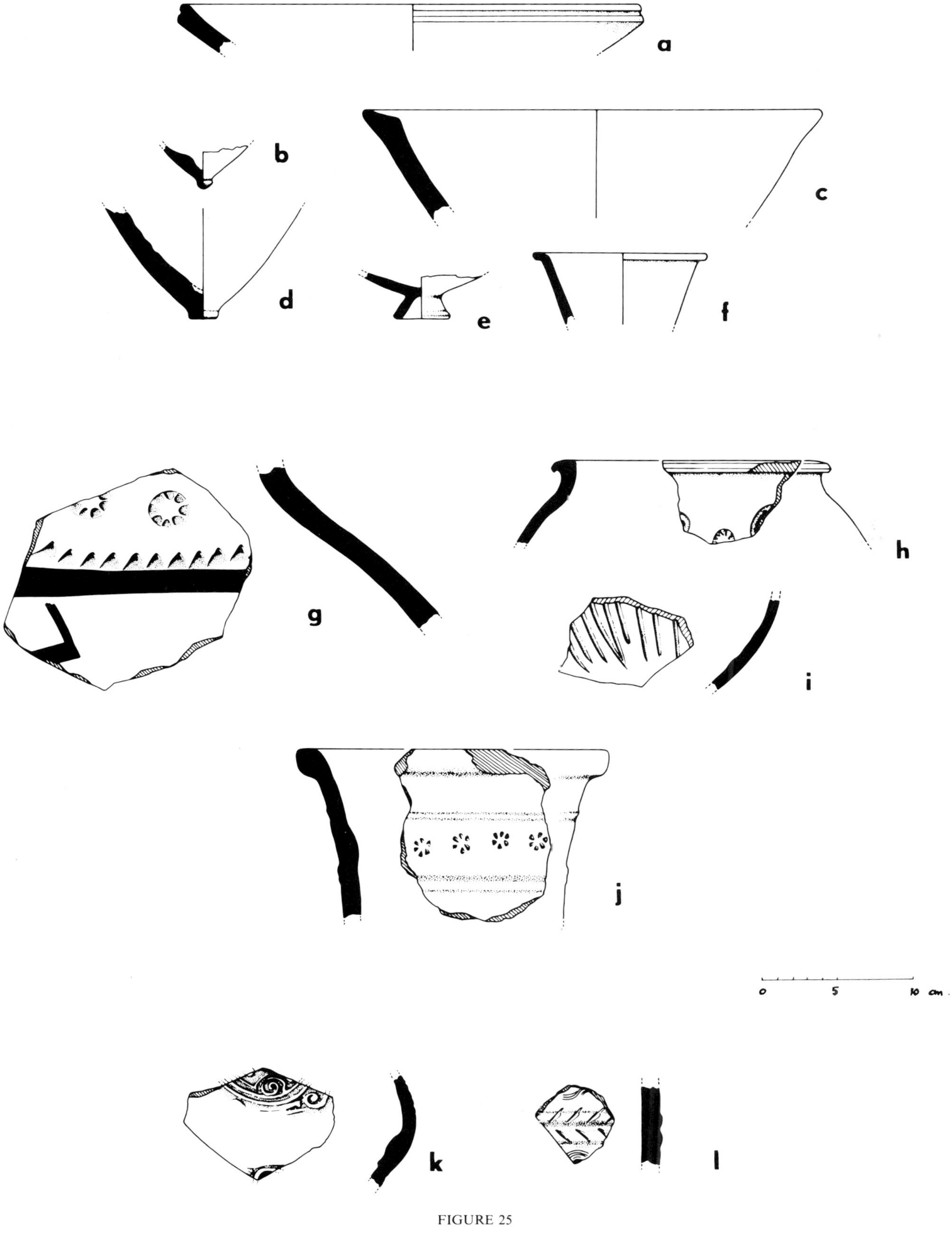

FIGURE 25

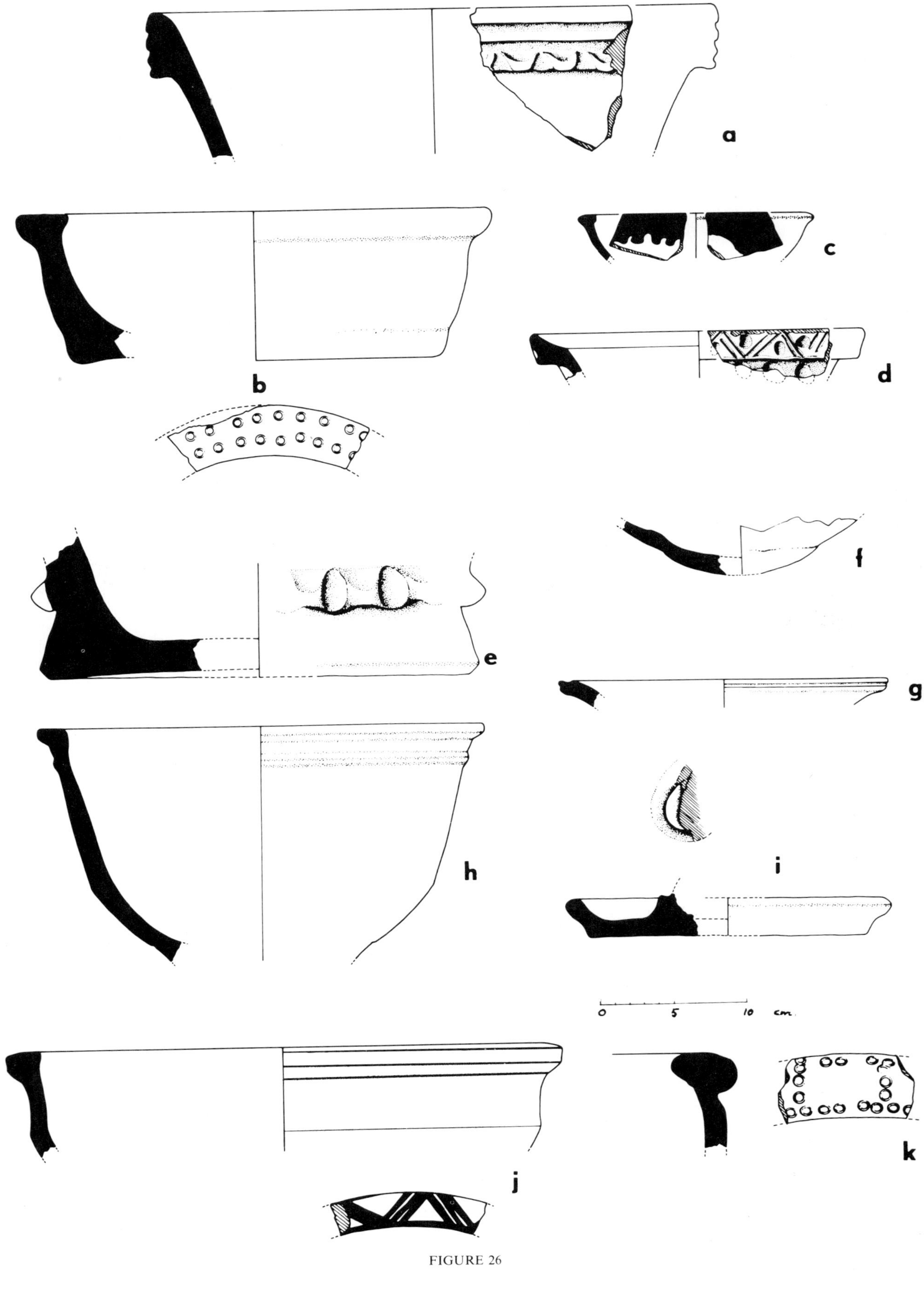

FIGURE 26

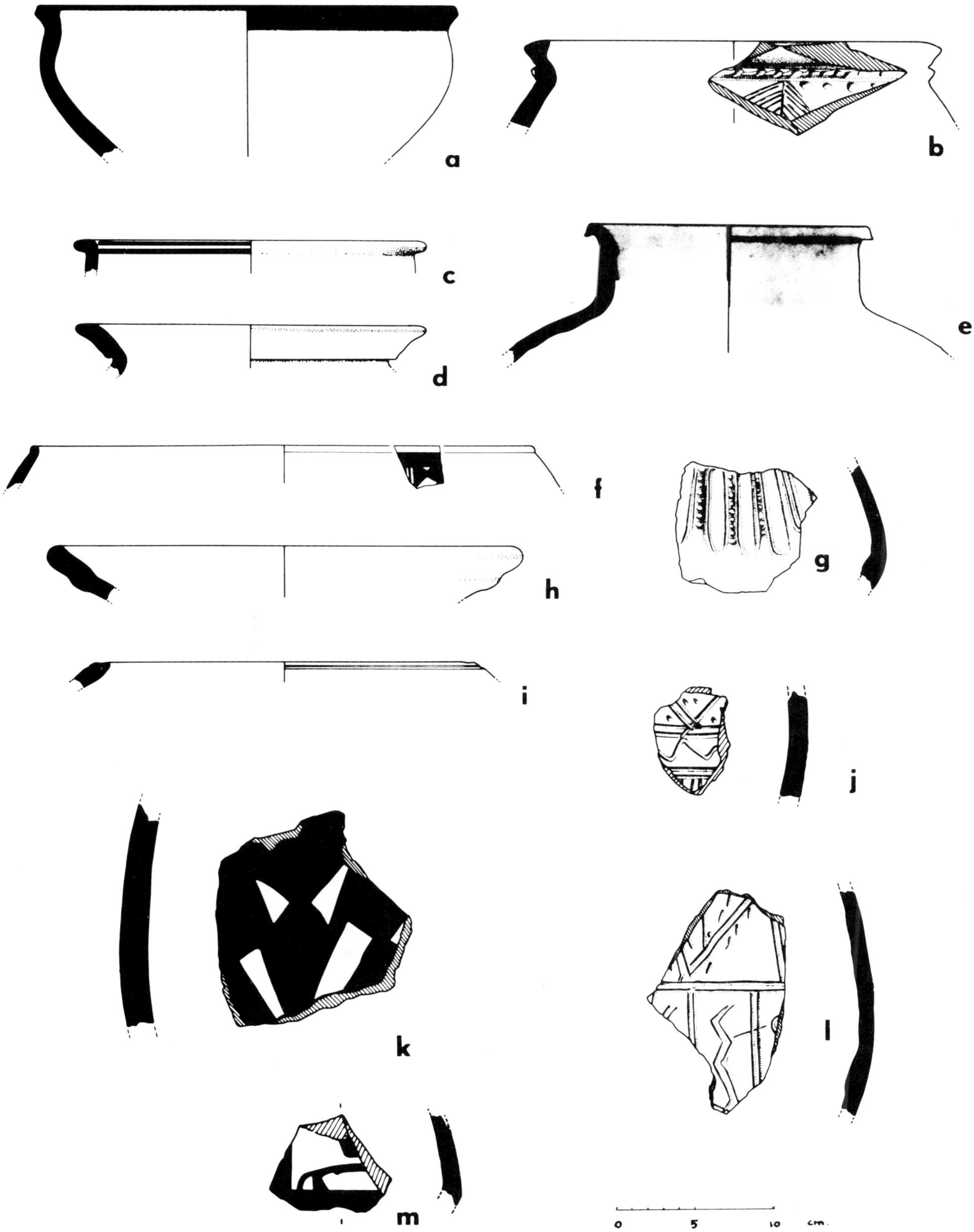

FIGURE 27

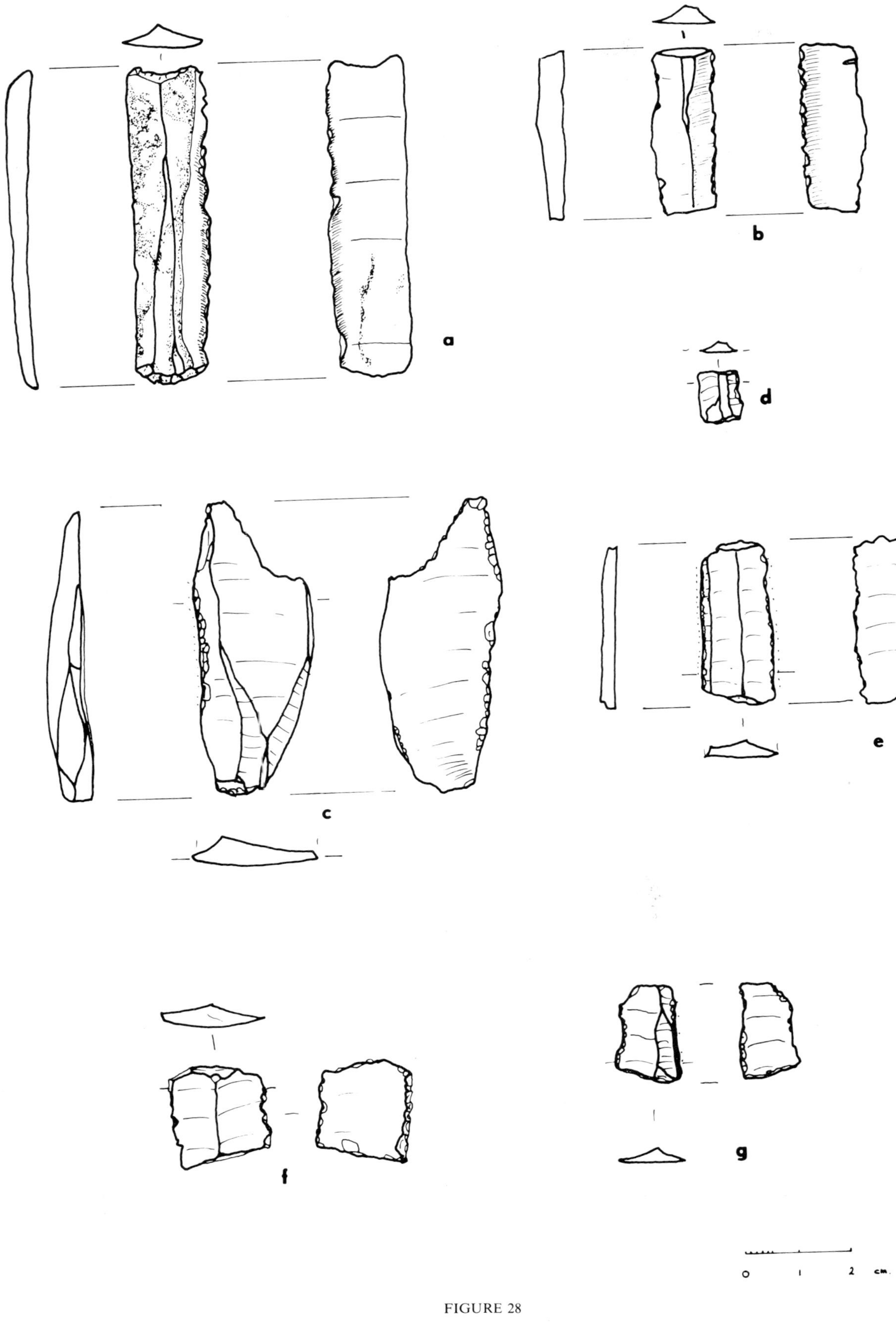

FIGURE 28

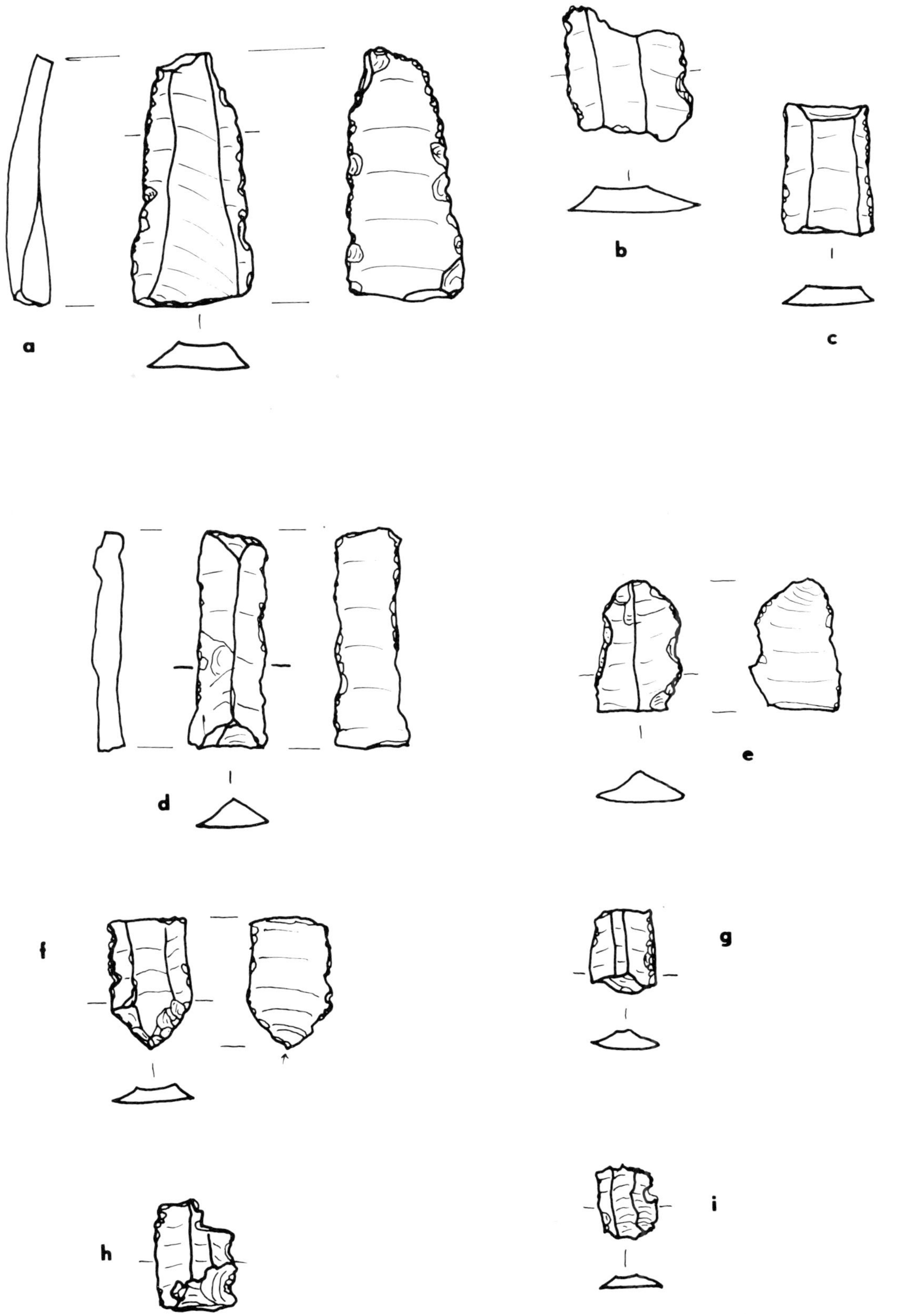

FIGURE 29

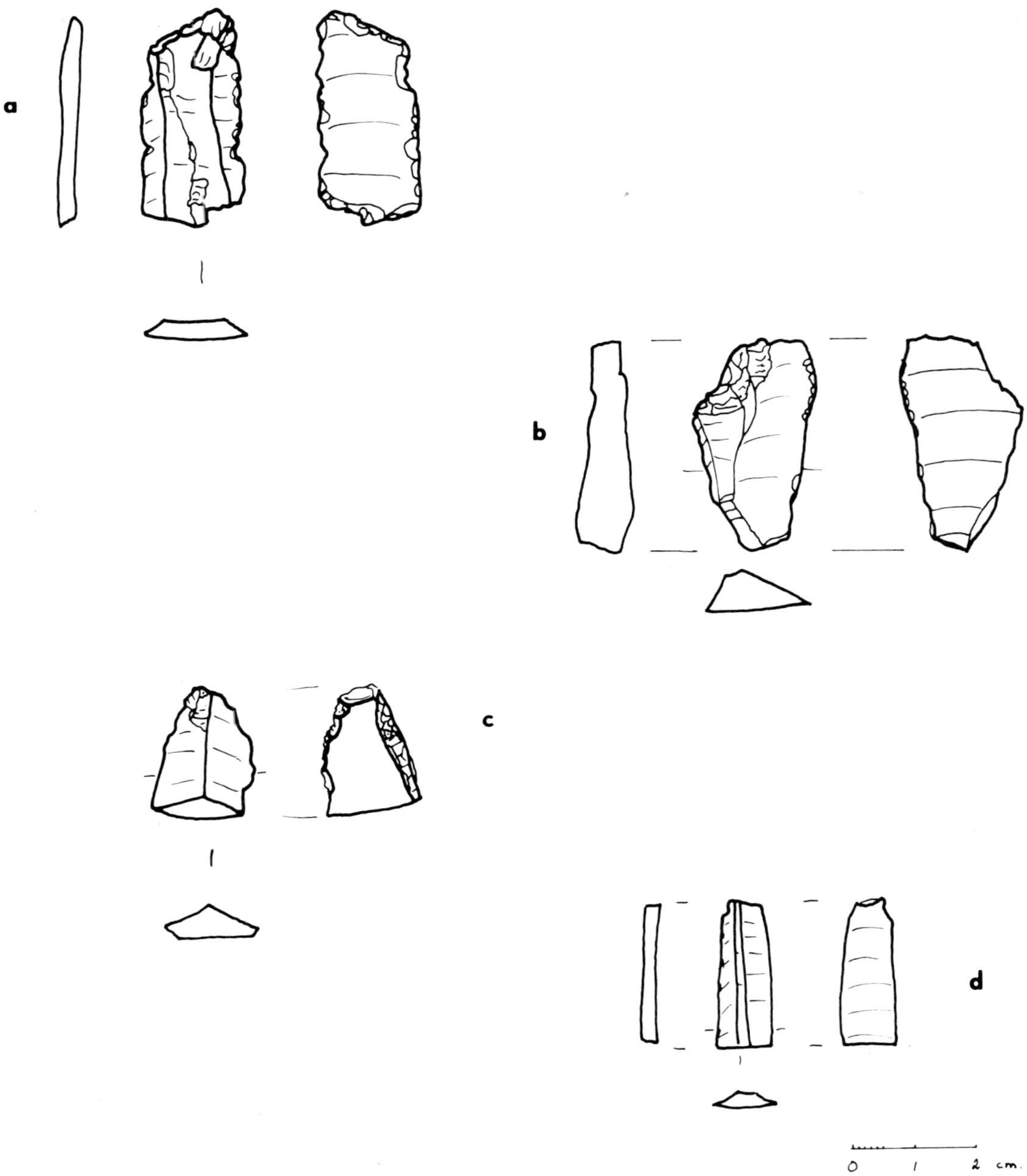

FIGURE 30

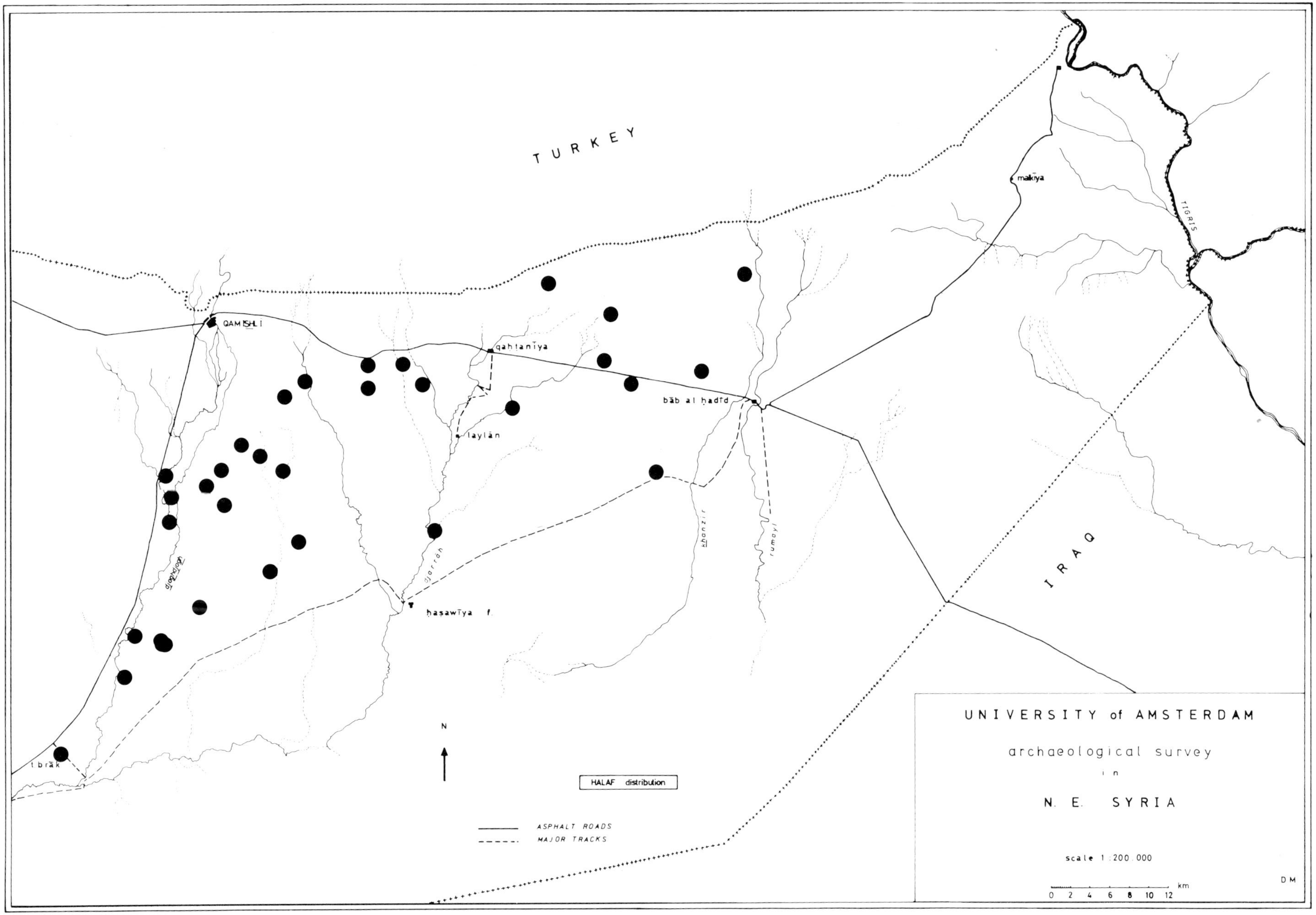
TURKEY
IRAQ
TIGRIS
malkīya
QAMISHLI
qahtanīya
laylān
bāb al hadīd
hasawīya f.
djarrah
khanzir
rumayl
tbrāk
N
HALAF distribution
ASPHALT ROADS
MAJOR TRACKS
UNIVERSITY of AMSTERDAM
archaeological survey
in
N. E. SYRIA
scale 1:200.000
0 2 4 6 8 10 12 km
D M

FIGURE 31

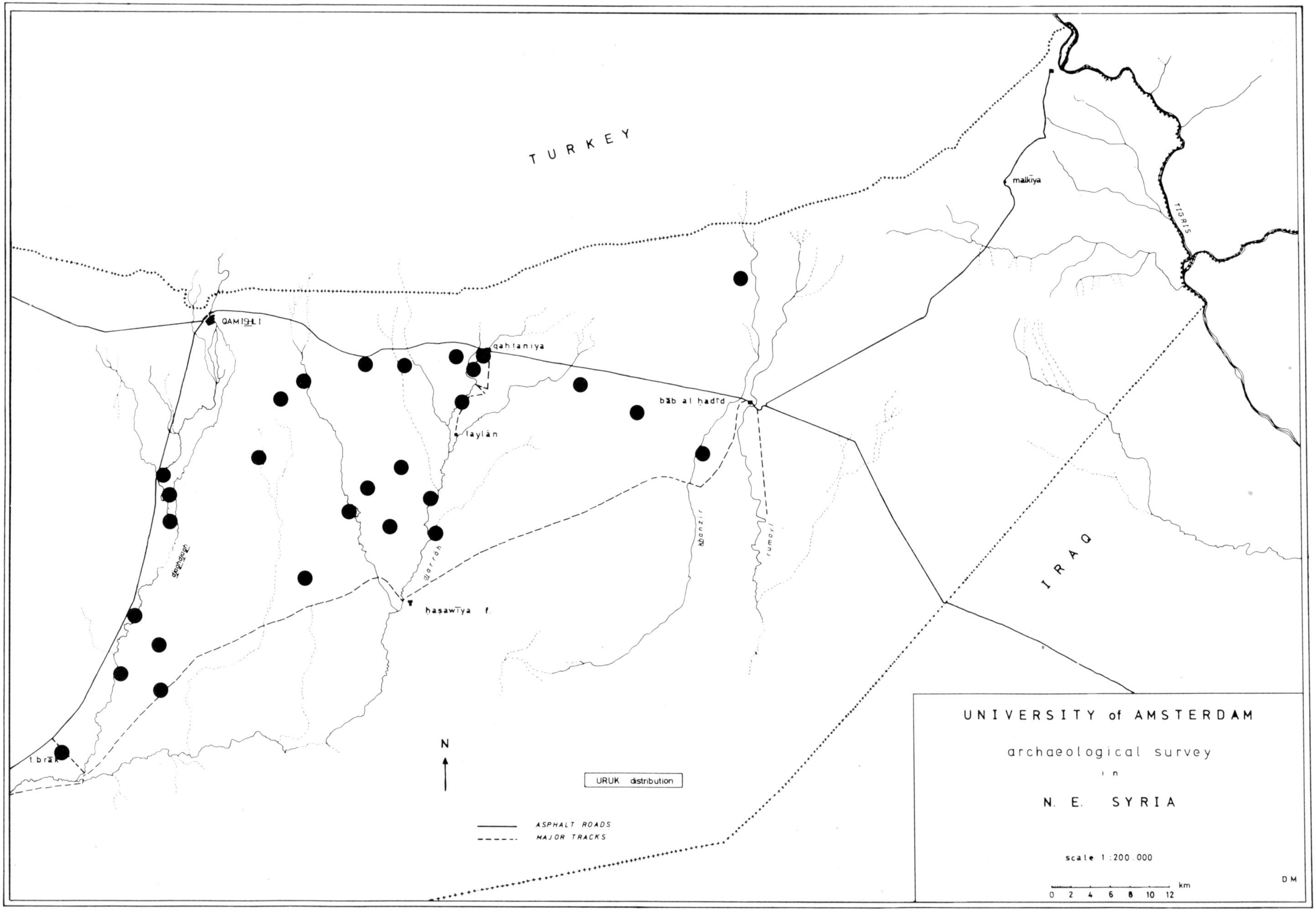
TURKEY
IRAQ
TIGRIS
malkiya
QAMISHLI
qahtaniya
laylān
bāb al hadīd
hasawīya
khanzir
rumayl
jarrah
jaghjagh
t.brāk
N
URUK distribution
ASPHALT ROADS
MAJOR TRACKS
UNIVERSITY of AMSTERDAM
archaeological survey
in
N. E. SYRIA
scale 1:200.000
0 2 4 6 8 10 12 km
DM

FIGURE 32

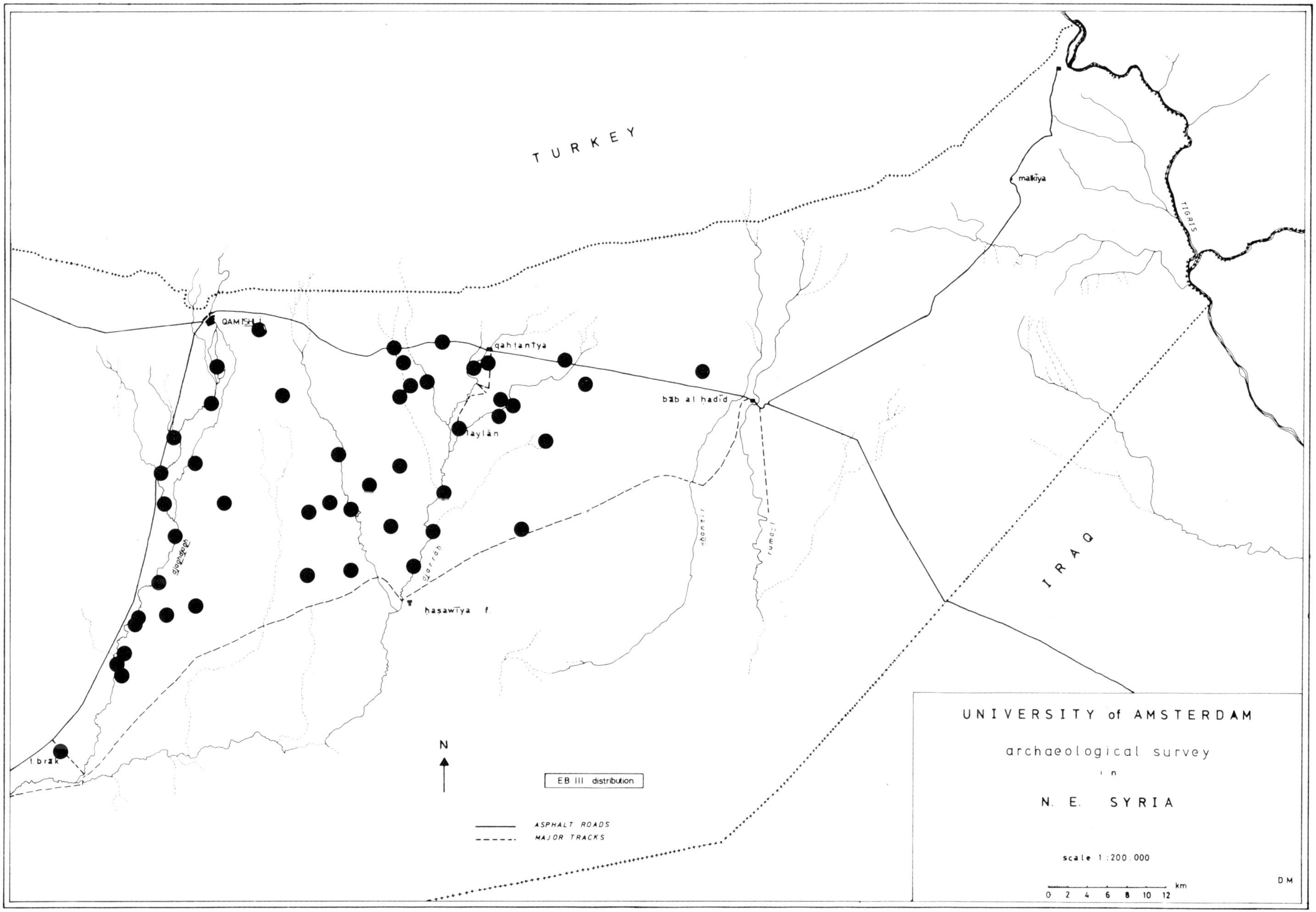
TURKEY
IRAQ
TIGRIS
malkiya
QAMISHLI
qahtaniya
laylan
bab al hadid
hasawiya f.
t brak
N
EB III distribution
ASPHALT ROADS
MAJOR TRACKS
UNIVERSITY of AMSTERDAM
archaeological survey
in
N. E. SYRIA
scale 1:200.000
0 2 4 6 8 10 12 km
DM

FIGURE 33

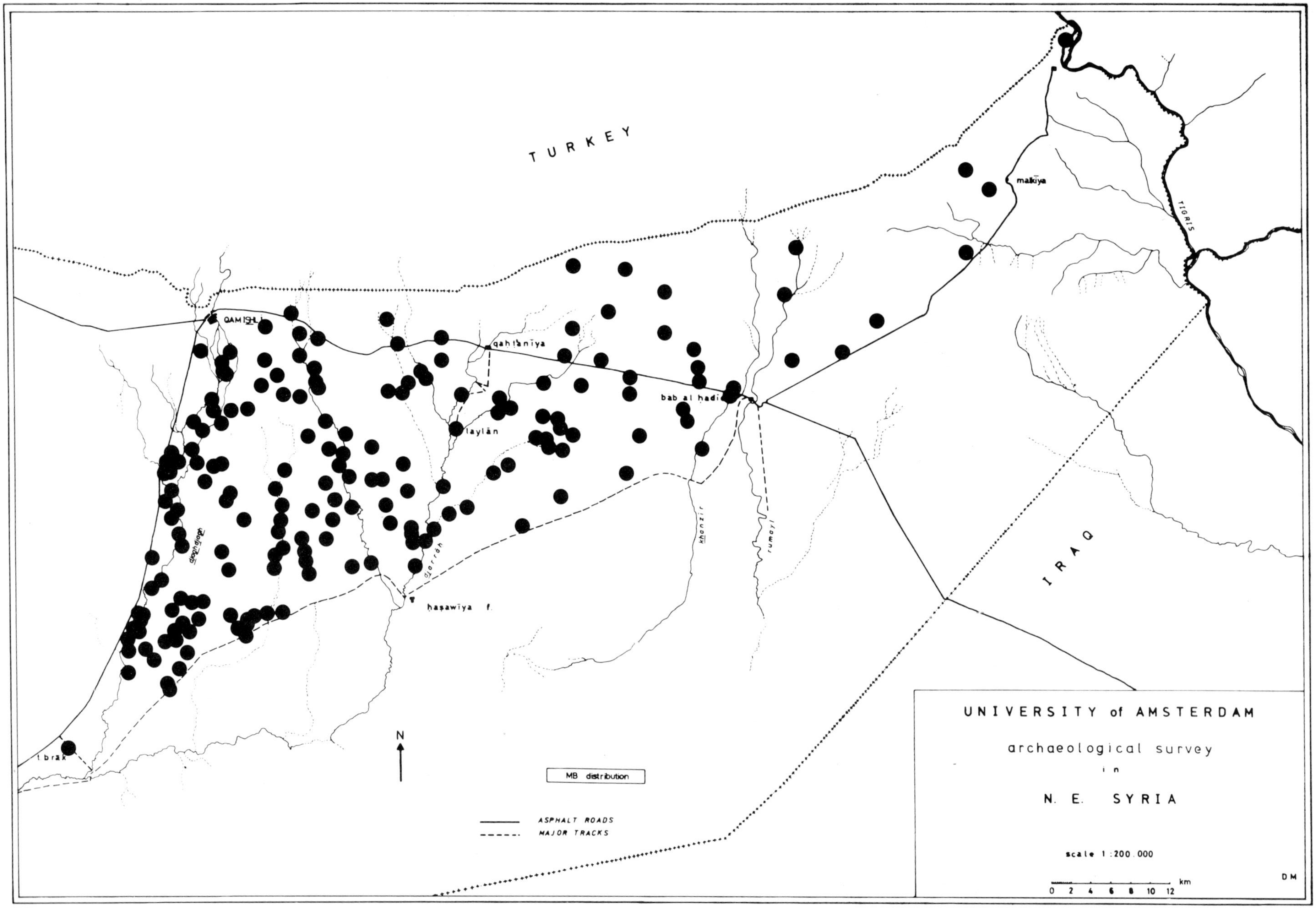
TURKEY
IRAQ
QAMISHLI
qahtaniya
laylān
bab al hadi
malkiya
TIGRIS
djaghdjagh
djarrāh
khanzir
rumayl
hasawīya f.
ibrāk
N
MB distribution
ASPHALT ROADS
MAJOR TRACKS
UNIVERSITY of AMSTERDAM
archaeological survey
in
N. E. SYRIA
scale 1:200.000
0 2 4 6 8 10 12 km
DM

FIGURE 34